Back from the Brink

A Christian COVID-19 Survival Story

Dr. Darrin Wilcox, PhD

Contents

This book is first and foremost dedicated to Jesus Christ. He is the one who brought me back from the brink and I would not be alive otherwise. He also is the one who died on a Roman cross for my sins and rose again on the third day. I would not live eternally in Heaven with Him otherwise.

There are so many people to thank. I kept a list of the medical providers I encountered. I didn't use their names here for privacy reasons, but they know who they are. More importantly, God knows who they are. Thank you all. I am also thankful to all the people who prayed for me while I was in the hospital and at home recovering after. I am thankful for those willing to hear God's prompting to pray for me in my moment of dire need and even to be anointed with oil and prayed over on my behalf. I am thankful to all my family and friends. Mostly, I am thankful to my wife, Melissa. It was she who nursed me back to life after I left the hospital. It was she who helped me become a man again after the calls for daily updates had ceased. Thank you.

Preface

This is a Christian COVID-19 survival story. I know what you're thinking, and you're right. We have moved past COVID-19 in policy and certainly in thought, but I encourage you to focus less on the COVID-19 part and more on the survival part. To be perfectly honest, on the spectrum of COVID-19 survival stories, mine is probably closer to the sniffles and high fever variety than the months in a hospital variety. My wife would likely take exception to that last statement, but as I've heard people tell their stories over time, mine sounds like a walk in the park. At the time, however, it was no walk in the park for me or my family. It was scary for many reasons, and we are still dealing with the impact nearly two years later. I have a feeling we will never fully recover from that time in our lives. Hopefully, we will never forget the lessons we learned.

In October of 2021, I spent 11 days in the hospital suffering from Covid Pneumonia. I spent about half of that time in the Intensive Care Unit. By the grace of God, I never had to be placed on a ventilator. But, as you will learn later, I was hours away from that reality and didn't even know it. In that moment, Jesus did something miraculous in my life. He didn't miraculously heal me, although I asked for that. I even tried to convince Him it would be such a powerful testimony for me just to get up and walk out of that place completely healed. He didn't buy it. Instead, he empowered me to fight for my own life and for the opportunity to return to those I love. No, I didn't spend months in a hospital. No, I wasn't placed on a ventilator for weeks on end. No, I didn't have to go to physical therapy to recover fully from my ordeal. Still, mine was a harrowing experience.

For much of my adult life, I have felt like God wasn't overly concerned with what I was doing and where I was doing it. That isn't to say He didn't care or that I wasn't seeking His will. It just felt like He was saying, "You can live here...or there. You can do this...or that. Just be ready when I call." And how does He call people when it's time? Sometimes He appears in a burning bush, sometimes He sends an angel, and sometimes He lets you go to the hospital ICU with COVID-19. In that moment, thinking shifts. You see that while you were chasing dreams and living adventures, He was preparing the way for you to fulfill His mission. In a place of trauma, you meet Jesus in a way you never had before. Perhaps, in that place, He brings you back from the brink of death. He might give you an exciting, new testimony to replace that old, boring one. Maybe He will teach you some fresh lessons for life. That's what happened to me. This is my COVID-19 survival story.

Chapter One

Back from the Brink

My Boring "Old" Testimony

So, here's a question for you. How excited are you about your salvation testimony? Seriously, be honest. I know every testimony of a life surrendered to Christ is exciting and powerful in Heaven, but on earth, where we put a premium on pizzazz, does it feel like some testimonies are more interesting than others? Some get your attention and even bring a tear to your eye, but others sound like a broken evangelical record.

My testimony never had the sorrow of years spent ruining my life with drugs. My testimony didn't have a miraculous healing from brain cancer. My course didn't change after an angelic visit, a powerful dream, or a vision of Jesus.

Nope. I grew up in church, mostly went to private Christian schools, attended Young Life every week, and hung around with other like-minded kids. As I got older, I never understood why many people with exciting, traumatic testimonies were a bit envious of...my testimony. While I'm thankful I've never been to jail or nearly died from a drug overdose, they had no idea just how boring it was growing up singing "Just as I Am" verses 1, 2, and 4 every Sunday. How could they be envious of me? Without the drugs and cancer and jail...I was actually jealous of them.

The first time I got saved, it was so boring I actually don't remember it. According to the inscription in my old Bible, it was sometime in 1976. I would have been six years old then and somewhere between kindergarten and first grade...the time when all good little church kids get saved. Please understand I am not being critical of the church or my formative years in the Bible Belt. Still, as I have looked back over my own Christian life, I have seen that so much of that "growing up in the church" life seems more about structure and tradition than salvation and testimony. No wonder it feels boring.

Depending on your variety of evangelical beliefs, I may have been saved that first time, or perhaps it was the second time...in 1981. By then, I was nearly 11 years old, and that experience was a bit more memorable. For that one, I recall the scene described in the Bible inscription. I was at our family church, at the steps leading up to the baptistry. The pastor was there with me, and we prayed together for me to receive Jesus Christ as my savior. Pretty standard stuff for a church kid. No near-fatal motorcycle crashes or strange illnesses, but I knew then, as I know now, that I was saved.

By 1981, I had been attending private Christian schools for a few years. At that time, it was a school associated with a fundamentalist Baptist church. I have memories of hair trimmed above the ears and off the collar (I actually once received a haircut from my 3rd-grade teacher behind the school the day of school pictures...my mom was not amused). I also recall the religious tracts in the small church bookstore...especially the one with depictions of people burning in the flames of hell (perhaps not politically correct in our time, but I got the message...not a place I wanted to go). And who can forget the weekly, mandatory chapel services? One of the few times in my life I received a paddling at school (yes, they used to do that...even in public schools, I would later learn) was a direct result of a boring chapel service. Another kid challenged me to see which of us could hit ourselves the hardest in the head with the spine of our Bibles. We went back and forth, with escalating intensity and increasing volume, until rudely interrupted by a teacher. To this day, I don't remember who won our little contest, but I can still feel the sting of that paddle on my back side.

I spent several years in that school, learning about the Bible and about God, even as I learned reading, writing, and arithmetic. It was a very formative time, and I am thankful that sacrifices were made so that I could be formed in a Christian environment. I learned much there, but it was all pretty standard for a church kid. It was shortly after another chapel service that the decision was made for me to change schools. During the last chapel before the summer break, the speaker encouraged us not to go off sinning during the summer break. You know, doing things like wearing shorts for boys or breaking the 11th Commandment...Girls shall only wear dresses. Even for good Southern Baptists, this was a little too far for my mom. I found myself at another Christian school when the next school year started. This time, however, the school was a bit more mainstream.

My sixth-grade year began at this new school with new opportunities to make friends. And that is exactly what I did. In fact, many of my closest friends today came from that time in my life. Even as I transitioned from private Christian school to public school in tenth grade, many of these friends transitioned alongside me. Yes, I am speaking of the great southern migration of boys from one private

Christian to one public school in the fall of 1985. Perhaps you have heard of it. Ok, probably not, but it made all the newspapers. Ok, that is not precisely true either, but we thought we were part of something important at the time. Why did we make the switch, you ask? To this day, I'm not exactly sure. At the time, it had something to do with experiencing the world outside the cocoon of Christian schools and a desire to go to a public university after high school. At the Christian school there was a lot of pressure to continue our educational journey at a private Christian university after high school, and after spending most of our lives in church kid world, who wanted to do that? So, we made the switch.

At this point, it would be fun to tell you that I started to walk on the wild side with my newfound public-school freedom. After all, these were the mean streets of public school, where hiding behind every open locker door was a bad kid offering you a beer and a cigarette. At least that was the warning when we left the comforts of the Christian school. While that wasn't even remotely accurate, I still found myself (with mental images of people burning in the flames of hell) becoming involved in Young Life and church-related activities. Joining me were the same Christian school friends that accompanied me to public school.

Throughout the balance of high school and into college (at a public university), that was my life. I moved from Young Life to Campus Crusade for Christ. Don't get me wrong, I risked the flames of hell with a beer among friends on occasion and even a cigarette or two, but I never got into the party crowd. I also didn't turn my back on my Christian heritage and education as I became more enlightened at the public university. My life was far from saintly, but on the spectrum of Christian kids, everybody's mom would have patted me on the head and praised me in front of their demon child.

I got married and started a family before finishing college. It might jazz up my old, boring testimony a bit to say I "had" to get married, but that wouldn't be the truth. I was young when I got married, but I was determined to break the cycle of divorce in my family. See, my mom and dad were married and divorced...twice. Sadly, I don't have any memory of either time. The first divorce happened around the time of my birth, and the second was when I was just a toddler. My mom remarried a divorced man. My dad had a couple of marriages in and around this time. The bottom line was that I knew divorce quite well. I was the private Christian school kid from a broken home. In those days, that was rare. I was determined to break that cycle for my own kid's sake and my own emotional well-being.

It didn't work. We called it quits after nearly eleven years of marriage and two kids. Actually, she called it quits, but that is another story. What I feared the most for my kids was now their reality...their lifelong reality. As divorce had impacted my entire life, even until this day, I knew what was in store for them. It broke my heart.

I moved back in with my mom and stepdad temporarily while I adjusted to the life of the Wednesdays and every other weekend dad. Up until that time in my life, I hadn't really experienced much loss. In fact, there was a joke in my grandfather's family that he and his siblings would live forever. With each passing family reunion, we all knew that one day the family's patriarchs and matriarchs would be gone. I knew that, as I got older, I would begin to experience the loss of loved ones. Up to that point, I had only lost my grandmother. Since she had health problems, the blow didn't carry a severe sting, but I knew the time would come for my beloved grandfather.

I wouldn't say the divorce turned out to be the bout with cancer or motorcycle crash that marks an exciting testimony, but it was a transformative time for me. During my marriage, I was a Deacon at the church, taught adult and children Sunday School classes, and even worked for the church as a pastoral intern. I led the men's ministry and the small group ministry. I went on a basketball (funny, since I'm not that tall and I've never been good at basketball) mission trip to Spain. I was well-known at the church and well-received in the Christian community in that area. By all accounts, I was doing everything a good Christian was supposed to do. From the outside looking in, I was really putting away that treasure in Heaven. But obviously, something was broken. One would think that something was a marriage or a family, but as I learned over the months and years that followed that something, for me at least, was my relationship with God. I had spent my life believing what I was taught, checking the Christian boxes, and trying to avoid the burning fires of hell. But did I really believe all that stuff? Did I believe it because I wanted to believe it? Was it MY relationship with God and not just some boring evangelical contract?

During this time, I deconstructed what I had always thought I believed and reconstructed my true belief from the ground up (in fairness, I am still reconstructing it). I knew I was saved, but what else did I really have? Winning a sword drill at Sunday School did not garner as much favor with God as we were taught to believe. Attending church every Sunday might look good on your church resume, but did it get you any closer to God? Christian schools, Young Life, bible studies, mission trips, prayers over meals, and everything else that goes along with being a good Christian had more to do with expectations of the local church than with a truly meaningful relationship with God. To put it succinctly, I had spent my life building a mediocre church resume instead of giving my life fully to Christ. And I had a boring testimony to prove it.

While this time in my life changed me for the better in so many ways, I can't say that this was the time I firmly grasped my testimony for Christ. I started reading my Bible more...really reading it...devouring it. I started praying more. I did a lot more spiritual self-reflection. I began having ongoing conversations with God. No, I didn't hear His audible voice (that would be awesome testimony material), but He would challenge me and direct me through my own internal voice. After a while, I got connected with a church again. I felt a little burned because my previous church didn't spring into action in my moment of need. As a matter of fact, I suddenly felt like I had leprosy. But that is a story for another time also. I was learning to trust God, but I needed to learn to trust His people again, also.

In 2005, I met and married the love of my life. We have two kids together. I am now the very proud father of four children and grandfather of a small but growing pack of grandchildren. We have been through much in our nearly eighteen years of marriage. In the early days, we dealt with the trauma of exes (mine), custody, courts, and tiny broken hearts. It was tough, but we watched God bless us abundantly in the midst of the shattered pieces. We have been blessed (and I credit my wife with the love and fortitude to make this happen) with strong, loving relationships between the older and younger kids. We have close relationships all around, actually. It really is a testament to the goodness and mercy of God. Things have not been perfect by any means, but we are happy.

We have also dealt with our share of family losses during our time together. The patriarchs and matriarchs of my grandfather's family finally started to pass away, including my own grandfather. My uncle, a father figure in my own life, also went to see Jesus. My wife lost her three remaining grandparents. And we have seen two beloved four-legged family members come and go. The sting of life and death is a painful reminder of our mortality and the risk that comes to anyone who dares to love.

Over the years, we have seen God move in mighty and miraculous ways in our lives. My youngest son had a brain issue in utero that was completely healed by the time he was born. We bought and sold a house at nearly the perfect time to enter and exit the market. We used the proceeds from that blessing to buy another house with cash. I got to do my dream job, not once but twice. I spent over twelve years in law enforcement (something I had wanted to do since I was a kid) before earning my Ph.D. and becoming a college professor. We have lived in several different states and have had many adventures we would not have had otherwise. In one move, God blessed us with housing in a market with no available housing. We have met people we would not have otherwise met. The blessings are too many to name, really. We are so very thankful. We are so humbled. We have seen so many miracles. And yet I still feel like my testimony is boring.

I know what you're thinking. How could I see so many miracles and blessings and still think my testimony is boring? How could God move so mightily and so often in my life, and I still think I have nothing to say? Why do I think drug addiction, brain cancer, motorcycle crashes, and angelic visits alone are the mark of a powerful testimony? Great questions, and the answer to each is that...I don't know. Honestly, it saddens me to think that I've always considered my testimony to be boring. When I take stock of all the many ways God has worked in my life (and in these words, I have recounted only a fraction of them), I feel that I have wasted much time NOT using my own story to impact the lives of others. How many people's lives could I have touched if only I had been obedient to use what God had given me to connect with them?

So, before telling the story of my "exciting, new" testimony, I want to encourage you not to overlook, diminish, and marginalize your own testimony. Maybe you can see yourself in some of the images I've described in this section. Maybe you have also doubted the power of your own broken evangelical record testimony. Perhaps you have passed opportunities by over the years because you just didn't think you had anything to say. Well, understand first that the same power that spoke the universe into existence can give your boring, old testimony a little pizzaz in the hearts of listeners. God really can impact the life of another with your stories of youth bible studies, behind-the-school haircuts from a 3rd-grade teacher at the Christian school, and years of sitting in the same pew at church. He doesn't need pizzaz to reach people. He really doesn't need your help at all. Sharing your testimony, even an old, boring one, is an opportunity and a privilege. It's one more way God gives you the joy of participating in His Kingdom work. Just give Him a chance to work through the boredom of your boring, church-kid, Christian life.

If only there had been someone to say these things to me over the years. Maybe there was, but I was so consumed with thinking my testimony was old and boring that I didn't listen. I don't know. But I now see that I was totally wrong. I just pray that God somehow reached the ones I passed by in that selfish place. It breaks my heart to think that my blindness to the things and ways of God might have been the difference in their eternal home. God, please forgive me.

Thankfully, the mercies of God never fail. He gives each of us the opportunity to start fresh and anew in the morning. We can choose to alter our life course on any day and at any time and surrender ourselves to His plans. And even though our old testimony is truthfully anything but old and boring, in His mercy, He decides to give you a new testimony. That is what He did for me.

As I have considered this new testimony, I have spent much time thinking of my old, boring testimony. In that place, I have realized that my old testimony isn't really boring at all. In fact, it flows seamlessly into my new testimony as the God story of my life up to this point. I know there will be new additions to my testimony in the future, but for now, God wants me to tell the story of this part of that journey. Remember that the story of any life surrendered to Christ is a powerful testimony. Hopefully, the story of this "new" testimony will impact you as it has impacted me.

Go West, Young Man

Contrary to many in my family, I have an adventurous spirit. When I was just 16, for instance, a friend and I made a whirlwind road trip to Peoria, Illinois (to visit a random girl he met at a Florida beach the previous summer), to St. Louis, Missouri (because her parents were not amused at our arrival and wanted us gone after the first night at their house), and then back home to Knoxville, Tennessee. In St. Louis, we rode to the top of the Gateway Arch and then visited Six Flags Over Mid-America. Honestly, I can't believe my mom let me do this (at least, I think I told her. Perhaps she is just now learning of this trip). Having kids of my own now, the thought of two 16-year-old kids traveling alone on such a road trip is just plain crazy. And yet, that's what we did.

I have always liked road trips and seeing new places. And I have always been fascinated with the western United States. One reason might be rooted in a classic American family RV trip to California a few years before the secret trip to Peoria, Illinois. My dad's dad lived in San Dimas, California, and we were headed out to see him. While California was wonderful, the best part of the trip for me was looking out the window at the passing western landscape. The dry desert landscape of New Mexico and Arizona gave me fantasies of wagon trains and wild west adventures.

It wasn't until many years later I learned that perhaps I came by this adventurous spirit honestly. While doing some family research, I discovered that my great-grandfather and my great-great-grandfather (both named Schuyler Wilcox, a name given to my youngest son) traveled west from Rhode Island to Nebraska in the mid to late 1800s in the early days of the Homestead Act period in our country's history. I even discovered a small, old book written by my great-great-grandmother about their adventures. Not satisfied with just one dangerous adventure to the deep mid-west, the book tells of their early-1900s adventure into the orange groves of California. Yes, this longing to see new things and go to adventurous places is in my DNA.

So, moving to Nebraska (a place I had only passed through once...earlier that year) in late 2019 to accept my first full-time teaching job at a community college made perfect sense. At least it made sense to me...my wife was not as convinced. Like many with an adventurous spirit, that drive for adventure can sometimes be reckless. My wife is the perfect balance to that potential for recklessness, as she would prefer one house, one neighborhood, one church, and preferably near family. But she is also supportive and humble, and though perhaps a bit reckless, we took off for Nebraska.

Most people who have never been to this part of the country consider it to be "fly-over" country. There may be some truth to that, but we discovered so much more. There is a rich western history there, and we were able to see many incredible things on the frequent day and weekend trips. We saw wagon-trail ruts from the 1800s carved into stone hills. We saw a stone-faced hill where adventurers traveling west carved their names and often, thankfully, the date. We saw beautiful Chimney Rock, used as a "highway marker" to those traveling further west in the wagon trains. In a bit of irony, we often now fondly talk of our time in Nebraska. We miss it. It wasn't completely reckless after all, but another western adventure awaited.

In the summer of 2020, we moved from Nebraska to the heart of Texas for a position at a 4-year private Christian university (some of you will catch the irony that I left the private Christian school many years before to avoid going to a Christian university and now I was to teach at one). As you will recall (and who can forget), this was during COVID-19. We didn't know it at the time, but we would soon discover that this new western adventure would turn out to be the miraculous providence of God.

"Sooner or later, everybody is likely to get COVID"

We were as frightened as the next person in the early days of the COVID-19 pandemic. We were still in Nebraska and found ourselves stocking up on canned foods (no, we didn't cause the toilet paper shortage). My wife and kids did not leave our apartment for the first three weeks after it was declared a pandemic. Classes at the community college had gone completely online, so I was at home. We did the grocery store pick-up thing, and I was the only one who left the house for the pick-up. After a few weeks, however, we started venturing out together more. It was becoming clearer that, while dangerous, COVID-19 could be mostly avoided with some common-sense safety practices. As more time passed and more information came out about the fatality rate, we found ourselves in the cautious but no longer frightened camp. We started living our lives normally, for the most part. We continued to go on adventures and looked forward to the promise of relief in the summer and fall (another expert opinion proved short-sighted).

School returned to in-class (with mandatory masking) status for the Fall semester of 2020 and then to voluntary masking for Spring 2021. We had gone back to normal, and while we knew people who had contracted COVID-19 (a couple with co-morbidities who had died), based on their experiences with the original strain, we were not overly concerned. I put applications out for a position at a 4-year university (I was now just weeks away from finishing my Ph.D.) and landed a position at a university in Belton, Texas. We were moving even further away from family. Initially, we had trouble finding a place to live (the housing market was going through the roof in Texas, Arizona, and Tennessee at the time). Still, God provided, and we found ourselves renting a lovely little house in a quiet neighborhood just minutes away from my job. I landed my dream job, and we were living in a fantastic part of the country (except for the summer heat). Despite a raging pandemic, it seemed like everything was coming together.

The original variant of COVID-19 had morphed into the Delta variant a few months earlier, and supposedly, this one was more dangerous. This variant was said to attack the lungs, causing more hospitalizations and even deaths. We watched as more people we knew got COVID, but again, based on their mostly minor cases, we were not overly concerned. We knew that it had been said everybody would eventually get COVID, but I was about half-way through my first semester at my dream job, and things were going pretty well. It was time for another day-trip adventure.

Caves and Coughs

In central Texas, they have this thing called "Cedar Fever". I had never heard of it, but apparently, the pollen from the cedar trees can cause flu-like symptoms. It impacts a lot of people, so as an outsider coming into this new environment, I wasn't surprised to catch Cedar Fever. The symptoms were similar to COVID-19 (what symptoms weren't at that time), and I investigated the differences out of an abundance of caution. Based on my investigation, it seemed that my suspicions were correct...I had Cedar Fever.

I felt a little off but not so much that we couldn't visit a nearby cave system for a little spelunking adventure (not like hard-core people with equipment and whatnot. This was more like suburban people on a guided tour through some caves, wearing shoes not quite appropriate for the mission). We had a nice post-spelunking lunch, but I was starting to cough by the time we got home. Apparently, Cedar Fever can be pretty rough, so I decided to head to bed early.

For the next several days, I missed work and felt increasingly worse. This was before the days of at-home COVID tests, and I didn't really feel like leaving the house and waiting in line somewhere for a test. Besides, I knew I had Cedar Fever. What was the point?

On October 15th, I had my wife drive me to a near-by medical clinic. I knew I had Cedar Fever, but I really needed something beyond acetaminophen and allergy medicine to knock it out. By this time, my breathing was a little off, and my head was feeling "swimmy," for lack of a better word. I figured they would have to do a COVID test, but knowing it would be negative, I just wanted them to give me something that would bring some relief from this horrible central Texas menace known as Cedar Fever.

By this point, you probably think I am a bit slow to the party on my COVID diagnosis, but I must say that I was a little shocked when they told me I was positive for COVID-19. Perhaps, I just didn't want it to be that. It wasn't that I was afraid of COVID. After all, my experience had mostly been one of knowing people with minor cases. Frankly, I just didn't want to be another number in some system and have to deal with the irritation of quarantines and doctor's notes and whatnot. It all just seemed like a real pain for people, not to mention now having to deal with the intrusion of the local health department in your life. Still, looks like I didn't have Cedar Fever after all. Wishful thinking...

I didn't know it then, but something happened at the medical clinic that would later prove critical. The nurse noted that my oxygen level was a little low while doing the standard diagnostic checks (temperature, blood pressure, etc.). Apparently, this level should be around 98 or 99 percent normally. Mine was about 93...after several tests. According to the nurse, this number was low but still within an acceptable range. In hindsight, I wish that more attention had been paid to that number then. As it was, however, I was sent home to rest after getting the prescription medications it would take to keep me less symptomatic while the COVID ran its course.

For the next several days, I got increasingly worse. My cough got worse. My head hurt worse. I just wanted to sleep all the time, and my wife said that sometimes I seemed a little "out of it. I didn't want to eat. I didn't want to get out of bed or off the couch. We didn't know it then, but that 93% oxygen level at the clinic had not improved.

My wife decided to order one of those finger pulse-ox gizmos from a large online retailer (you know which one I mean). I have to say that I have never been more grateful for next-day delivery (another of God's miracles in this instance). In fact, I'm not sure I would have made it another day or two without lapsing into a coma. Our pulse-ox arrived the next morning, and initially, we thought it was broken. It was reading in the high 70s and low 80s for me. There was no way this could be correct. My wife tried it, and even though we knew by this time that she likely had

COVID too, it read the normal 98 to 99 percent for her. Something wasn't right.

Like most men, I didn't want to believe this was happening, and I thought it would just work itself out. You know, maybe I could just walk it off. Rub some dirt on it. I felt too bad and too "out of it" to really think it through clearly. I kept going back and forth. Should I go back to the clinic? Should I go to the ER? Should we call an ambulance? Surely, this would just go away with a little more time. Surely my oxygen level would go back up, or we would discover that the pulse-ox didn't like me for some reason. That evening I asked my wife to call 911 for an ambulance, and so began a new adventure. This time it wasn't to Mount Rushmore or Roswell, New Mexico. No, this adventure would take me to the brink of death, where I would encounter Jesus himself and from which I would return with a brand-new testimony.

Picture of Death

On October 19th, I took my first ride as a patient in an ambulance. As a former police officer, I had ridden in plenty of ambulances but until that day, never as a patient. But I'm getting ahead of myself.

Within a few short minutes from the time my wife called 911, a firetruck and a rescue truck arrived. Another person arrived in a personal vehicle, which was well before the ambulance arrived. At this point, we began seeing God's hand at work. As we reflected later on this time in our lives, we saw His hand clearly at work in bringing us to Texas in the first place. More on that later.

As a police officer, I have been on many scenes with rescue personnel. I have never been on a scene like the one unfolding in my living room. After the fire and rescue personnel entered our house, the living room started to bust at the seams. There were a lot of them there. In addition to the firefighters, there was also a doctor. On this night, a doctor from the hospital was riding with the fire team. But that wasn't all. There was actually a second doctor there. This was the one who arrived in a personal vehicle. They were on call with the fire department that evening. And there is still more. Riding with the fire team that night was a med student. So, when I say the hand of God was at work, I'm being serious. He didn't just send some of the best firefighters I have ever met, He also sent 2 ½ doctors in my time of need. He is a very good God indeed.

No shock this time, but my oxygen level was still reading low. As a matter of fact, it was reading in the low 70s. My wife later told me that one of the 2 ½ doctors expressed surprise that I was not already in a comatose state. I didn't fully realize it at the time, but I was flirting with death and had been for several days. When they hit me with the oxygen, I felt better than I had in days. Actually, I felt so good that I figured this would do the trick. More than likely, I would be patched up in a short time and on the road to normalcy. Hearing that I needed to go to the hospital with them was a real punch in the gut. I know, I know...I'm not very bright, am I? Denial is a powerful force.

So, at this point, I was getting on a stretcher and getting strapped in for my ride to the hospital. I was feeling so good with the oxygen that I felt like myself again. I was joking with the firefighters and the ambulance personnel (they had arrived by this time). I was expressing my most sincere gratitude for their help. I almost didn't feel it when one of the firefighters started my IV before the ambulance arrived (I'm afraid of needles). I just knew that I was going to be in and out of the hospital in no time.

Still, I couldn't completely drive away thoughts of mortality. What if I never see my family again? What if I leave my children without a father (especially in the formative years for my younger children)? How could I leave my wife without a husband? What would she do now that I had moved us more than a thousand miles away from family? I need to make sure she knows where my life insurance information is. I need to make sure she knows all of our passwords for bills and savings accounts and whatnot. I'm feeling pretty good, and I'm pretty sure that I will be back home later...but what if I never make it back home? What if this is the last time I ever lay eyes on my family? What if this is the last time my children will ever see their father alive? Is this it, God?

Only later, after I got home, did I learn that my wife was having the same thoughts as they loaded me in the ambulance. What if I never see him again? Will my children lose their father at such a young age? What will I do without my husband? Why did you bring us so far away from family? All this emotion and fear was perfectly captured in a photograph my wife took as I was loaded into the ambulance. My children are looking through the glass storm door, watching their father being taken away. While you cannot see their faces in the photograph, their demeanor captures the trauma of this night for them. Will we ever see our dad again? That picture and others from this adventure can be viewed online at www.backfromthebrinkbook.com.

Right Place, Right Time Part 1

The ride to the hospital was uneventful. I was not an emergency case (not life and death at the moment), so we didn't even run with lights and sirens. No bother, really, as I had spent plenty of time doing that as a police officer.

Upon arrival at the hospital, the pace of things changed dramatically, though. It was then that I began to realize, perhaps, just why we came to Texas in the first place.

When we moved to Texas, I thought I had landed my dream job. I wanted to be a professor at a private Christian university in the criminal justice department. That's what I was doing. The people I was working with were marvelous, which was an added blessing. The thoughts of hot summers and long distances to family weren't pleasant, but we could and would make it work. I hadn't seen an angel or heard the audible voice of God, but I felt pretty sure that we were supposed to come to Texas. When the COVID ordeal was over, we were 100% sure of that...just for a different reason.

After being wheeled into a room in the ER, I encountered no less than ten different medical personnel. There were nurses and at least three different doctors, all scurrying around asking me questions, taking diagnostics, and getting me hooked up to a different, heavy-duty oxygen line. This one sounded like a jet engine and would remain with me 24 hours a day for days to come. They were all masked, and some double-masked due to the risk of COVID. One doctor even had a helmet on his head reminiscent of Apollo 11. I inquired about it, and he said he ordered it from Amazon. What a crazy time this pandemic turned out to be.

Everyone I encountered was nice. They were helpful. They were professional. And this was to be the norm throughout my time there...except for one ER nurse. He was helpful and professional but seemed to have grown weary of the pandemic at this point and was taking it out on me. But in a bit of irony, he was also the one God used to perhaps begin the process of saving my life. He was the one who finally told me when we were alone in the room during a break in the action that I was "very, very sick". He told me I was just beginning the fight for my life. I was feeling better getting oxygen and was still under the self-imposed, false impression that I would leave in a few hours. Now I didn't know if I was going to make it out alive. It was a sobering moment, and admittedly, I wanted to punch him in the face, but I also knew that I needed to hear what he had to say. I needed to get ready for the fight. Perhaps God had brought us all the way to Texas for this fight. As I pondered his warning, I thought that we could not be in a better place. For the past several years, we had lived in places that just didn't have the medical resources we had here. I didn't ask for this fight. I didn't want this fight. But perhaps this was the right place and right time.

I didn't know it yet, but I later learned that God had even "stacked the deck" a bit in my favor for this fight.

The Place They Take You to Die

I was still in a state of shock as they wheeled me up toward the Intensive Care Unit. The flurry of activity had ended in the ER. I had my first CT scan in my life. And now it was just me and two nurses attired like I had the black plague.

When we arrived on the ICU floor and began rolling toward the doors, I thought we had entered a construction zone. There was thick plastic draped everywhere, especially covering any tiny cracks or holes keeping the "plague" in the ICU and out of the remainder of the hospital. The doors were covered in plastic, and large, ominous signs were posted, warning that the area beyond those doors was secured and nobody was to enter without authorization. It was deathly quiet just outside those doors, and my heart sank just a little as the doors were opened and we crossed the threshold.

The deathly silence just outside the ICU doors gave way to beeping machines and workplace chit-chat as they wheeled me toward my section of curtained-off ICU space. My heart sank even more deeply as I looked around and realized that, aside from the medical staff, I was the only conscious person in the room. They wheeled me into my little area, and suddenly the sound of beeping machines and workplace chit-chat became almost unbearably loud. As I started to fully ingest the gravity of my situation, a tear formed in the corner of my eye, and I thought to myself... "this is the place they take you to die."

The Healing Power of Fruit

I like most fruit, but I don't eat much fruit. This changed during my time in the hospital and when I arrived home afterward. It also served as a reminder of the power of the Fruit of the Spirit, as described in the Bible.

I hadn't really eaten in several days due to my "Cedar Fever." Now that I was feeling a little better from the constantly pumping oxygen machine, I started feeling a bit hungry. In fact, I was feeling starved, but as one can imagine from my description above, they don't send meals up to the place where everybody is sedated and on a ventilator. I asked the nurse if there was anything to eat up there. By this time, it was getting pretty late and well past dinner time. She said she would have to scrounge around but didn't have high hopes for a complete meal. She returned a little later with two packs of saltine crackers (restaurant style with two crackers per pack) and two small fruit cups. It would have to do.

I can't say it was the best meal of my life, but it was pretty high on the list at that moment. As I finished off the second fruit cup, I found myself thinking about the Fruit of the Spirit from Galatians 5 in the Bible. In his letter to the Galatians, the Apostle Paul contrasts the acts of the flesh with the Fruit of the Spirit. Paul describes a person guided by the flesh as one who, among many things, is envious, full of hatred, angry, and selfish. Such a person, Paul says, will not inherit the Kingdom of God. This is not because they have done bad things. Who among us has not? Instead, this is because these things are a picture of the condition of their heart. Missing from their heart is God.

On the other hand, a person filled with the Spirit of God demonstrates the Fruit of God's Spirit through love, joy, peace, patience, kindness, goodness, faithfulness, gentleness, and self-control. Paul says that there is no law against such things. These things are the mark of someone whose heart is filled with God.

Throughout my life, I have seen myself more closely aligned with the person guided by the flesh. To be sure, I have counted myself "saved" from a young age, but my daily life has often been lived out in envy, hatred, anger, and selfishness. There have been moments, glimpses of those fruits, but to say that they have marked my life would be a stretch. And yet, as I pondered Galatians 5 and finished off my fruit cup, I realized that, by God's grace alone, I had been marked by those Fruit since this unwanted adventure began.

Until my wife called 911 and the firefighters arrived with their blessed oxygen, I had been pretty out of it. Indeed, I felt much better after getting that oxygen, but I didn't "come to my senses" angry and selfish. In fact, my wife later said it was almost alarming how "not grumpy" I was. From that moment until well after my recovery at home, I found myself being thankful, patient, at peace, loving, gentle, and so on.

It wasn't intentional on my part at the beginning, but as I had the opportunity, I sincerely thanked each medical staff member for helping me. Whenever someone entered my area to take my blood pressure, prick my finger, give me a shot in the stomach, adjust my airflow, deliver my meal, or take out the trash, I thanked them with much sincerity and heartfelt love for what they were doing. I asked their names and tried to remember them, so I could greet them by name when they returned. I showed interest in them. I didn't treat them like this was their job, and they should be happy to have one, but instead like they were demonstrating love and service to me through their "job." I loved every one of them, but it was not through my own heart of flesh. Instead, it was through the power of the Spirit of God found in a cup of fruit.

I later learned that I was the favorite patient in the ICU. Granted, since I was the only conscious patient in the ICU, the competition was slanted a bit in my favor, but it warmed my heart nonetheless to hear. It seemed that the hospital staff found me to be thankful, gracious, loving, gentle, peaceful, kind, and full of joy in a bad situation. I had heard other patients in nearby rooms after I was moved out of the ICU. Some of them, like me, were recovering from COVID-19. One of them, I later discovered, was not doing well at all. He would scream and curse loudly both day and night. He was not thankful, gracious, gentle, kind, or peaceful. My heart went out to him, knowing his pain and fear. I prayed for him in my heart. The medical staff was not eager to endure his wrath, and he was later moved because he was disturbing others. I never learned how his COVID-19 story ended.

By God's grace, I continued to demonstrate the Fruit of the Spirit throughout my time in the hospital, and apparently, it continued to shine a little light into a dark place for the people I encountered. I can't say if somebody's life changed, and of course, I would take no credit if it had, but God has called His children simply to sow seeds. We may never see what happens to the plant. That is entirely

God's business, but He does give us the good pleasure of demonstrating the Fruit of His Spirit if we will only agree to be His vessel.

I wish I could say my life since this time was marked daily by the Fruit of the Spirit, however, I still find myself angry, envious, and selfish at times. But I did take that life lesson on demonstrating those Fruit home with me after leaving the hospital, and it is something I ponder often. I pray that I will increasingly surrender my heart of flesh to the Fruit of the Spirit. It's a daily journey, but I will never forget seeing firsthand the power of those Fruit and how what I found in the bottom of a simple cup would bring even a short-lived smile to the faces of others.

Thankfully, I discovered the healing power of both a fruit cup and the Fruit of the Spirit shortly after arriving at the ICU. But, as evening turned into that first night, I saw firsthand just why this was "the place they take you to die."

You Want Me to Be Selfish!?

One would imagine a large room full of sedated people would be quiet at night. That could not be further from the truth. Apparently, when your patients are sedated and unaware, there is no compelling reason to be quiet. The beeping of machines and the constant chatter of medical staff made sleeping difficult. At this point, I was exhausted, yet the fear of the unknown and the noise of the ICU kept me from getting the sleep I so desperately needed.

Since I was on a roll with the Fruit of the Spirit thing, what better activity to engage in while remaining sleepless than to pray for my sedated ICU comrades. I didn't know them. I didn't know their names. Except for the ability to catch a glimpse of one comrade through a slit in the curtain, I could not even see them. Still, I prayed. I prayed, and I prayed. With silent tears accompanying silent prayers, I prayed for them with all I had.

I saw an older black man through that slit in the curtain. I could barely see his face, and in a bit of irony, I thought he was our neighbor from across the street (we hadn't seen him for a few weeks), but I learned the next day this was not my neighbor. I prayed for him in earnest. I prayed for his healing. A miraculous healing. I prayed that he would get up and walk out of there completely healed. I prayed he would do that, leaving me behind. Yes, I wanted out of there, but the prayers I found myself praying came from a place of complete selflessness. It wasn't really like me.

It was now late at night, but I still could not sleep. I was beyond exhaustion from the experience and the praying, and it was at this point that God taught me another valuable Kingdom lesson. At first, I thought I wasn't hearing the Lord right. There was no way He was directing me to be selfish. After all, selfishness was not a Fruit of the Spirit but a sign of the flesh. How could He be telling me now to stop praying for others? How could He be telling me instead to think about myself?

I obeyed at that moment, but I didn't understand what was being said until later. I felt the Lord telling me to stop praying for others. I sensed Him saying that He really appreciated my efforts (tongue in cheek a bit, as He could certainly do things without them) but that I had a fight ahead of me and I needed to instead focus on...me.

Since my very first Sunday School felt storyboard lesson, I have been taught that, as Christians, we sacrifice ourselves for others. I learned a maxim early on: "Jesus first, others second, me last." How could I reconcile those lessons with a direction to be selfish?

Well, the answer is that it wasn't a direction to be selfish but instead to engage in what we might term "self-care" today. "Oh, surely not," you say. "The Lord would never call us to something like that." Are you sure? Matthew 22:39 tells us to love others as ourselves. Assumed there is that we...love ourselves. Of course, you could also take it to mean as we would *like to be loved*, but personally, I can't argue away the crazy notion that God does want us to love ourselves. And part of loving yourself is caring for yourself...self-care. God was simply telling me, "Hey, I've got these other folks. Thank you for praying for them in earnest. Now, *stop* praying for them and focus on yourself. You have a fight ahead of you, and it's just now starting. Focus on...you."

I had spent over 50 years on the earth at this point. I spent most of those years in church, Christian school, and Bible studies, and this was the first time I remember understanding that it was ok to focus on myself. To love me. So, that is what I did. I left my ICU comrades in the hands of God and began to pray for me. At first, my prayers were straight out of the New Testament. It would be an incredible testimony to miraculously stand up, COVID-free, and walk right out of that ICU. As I walked out the sealed doors, I would say loudly for all to hear that Jesus had completely healed me and that if they had never thought much about Him before, they probably should now. Wow! How awesome! How amazing! What a testimony! And yet, not the testimony I was being given. With fresh tears, I finally slipped into a restless sleep.

Night From Hell

I have awakened many times over the years to a loud, annoying alarm clock. In the early days, it wasn't the more pleasant alarm sounds now found in most smartphones.

No, it was the scare you half to death, heart racing for several minutes type of sound. You "older" folks know what I'm talking about. That is the type of sound that awakened me now.

I had seen hospital shows before, with the beeping sounds of low oxygen or time for some medicine or even a stopped heart. But I had never heard them with my own ears. As a police officer, I had seen plenty of dead people, but I usually wasn't there in the final moments. I wasn't there with the loud, annoying, blood-curdling, heart-racing beeps and alarms. Apparently, my restless sleep had morphed into a deeper sleep. After being startled awake, it took me a minute or so to realize where I was. I wasn't at home. I wasn't in my own bed. That's not my alarm. Dangit! I guess this wasn't all a really, really bad dream.

The sounds of death in a hospital are blaringly loud yet eerily silent. I couldn't see this impending death, but the sounds of beeping machines, even louder voices, and scurrying bodies were unmistakable. I hadn't really gotten a good look at my ventilated neighbors when I arrived, but from the sound of things, it was a neighbor two or three "rooms" down. I had no idea who this person was. I didn't know if it was a male or female. Young or old. Father. Mother. I didn't know anything about them other than they were apparently dying. And perhaps that's what happens to everyone up here, including me.

The sounds became more still after 30 minutes or so. The voices got quieter again. The bodies were no longer scurrying. And yet it was not the sound of death. It was the slow, faint, rhythmic beeping of a beating heart. I know I wasn't supposed to be praying for anyone, but I couldn't help but pray for this unknown comrade during those 30 minutes or so. Whoever they were, they would go on to live and laugh and love and be loved. And yet this night from hell was only just beginning.

After another round of being startled awake, loud voices, and scurrying bodies, it was apparent that the prognosis for this person was not good. I heard one end of a quiet conversation on the telephone, and within an hour, I heard the distinctive sounds of an arriving, soon-to-be crushed family.

It turns out my comrade was a man. I heard a weeping, tearful woman call him "dad." The only thing worse than the sounds of death are the sounds of someone saying "goodbye" to someone they love. The medical staff had brought "dad" back twice, but they knew he wouldn't make it through the night. His lot was to become another death statistic in the daily reporting of COVID-19 numbers. I wept silently in bed as I heard his family tearfully say "goodbye." I thought of my own family and how I hoped beyond hope that they would not soon be ushered through the sealed ICU doors to say "goodbye" to me. I couldn't help but pray for that daughter and whoever else was saying "goodbye" that night. I was exhausted again from lack of sleep and praying, and I felt the Lord compelling me to save my strength. As the Emergency Room nurse told me, the Lord was telling me now, I was in for the fight of my life...literally. I somehow drifted off to sleep listening to the quiet weeping of a near-fatherless daughter.

"I'm Not Dead Yet"

I awoke early in the morning. This was a habit I was to enjoy (not so much my wife) throughout my time in the hospital and during my recovery at home. With the thoughts and sounds of the previous night still in my head, I relished the discovery that I wasn't dead yet. But I still found myself in the place they take you to die, and I was growing concerned that it was just a matter of time before I was sedated and ventilated. It was just a matter of time before my family received that late night call to come and say "goodbye" to me.

As I waited for the doctor to arrive, a nurse entered my curtain-room with breakfast. I learned it was a bit of a special request, as hospital staff didn't usually bring breakfast up to this area. I can't say I remember what I had for breakfast that morning, but I do remember the fruit. From here on, I would look forward to that fruit with most every meal. The fruit became a source of comfort and routine for me, physically and spiritually.

According to the doctor, my vitals were good, and my oxygen level was holding. I had grown somewhat accustomed to the jet engine around my neck pumping oxygen into my nostrils. I didn't know what the numbers meant in terms of my oxygen level (does a doctor ever actually explain something well to lay people?) but I did understand that I wasn't looking at a ventilator yet. I was in good spirits, but I didn't know if I could take another night in the hall of curtains.

That day was fairly uneventful. I got to know my nurses a bit and found one of them easy to talk to. She said that it was actually nice to talk with a patient up here. In this place, the patients were almost all sedated. I was sad to see her go when it was time for shift change, especially as evening was approaching, and I was starting to dread the thought of the beeps and scurrying and tearful goodbyes of another night.

I barely got to meet my new nurse when she advised me that they now had a private room in the ICU for me. I would be moved down the hall to that room shortly, which in hospital time turned out to be about 2 hours. Nevertheless, I was relieved when the brakes on my bed were lifted, and I could put the visions of ventilated patients in my rear-view mirror. As they moved me into my new room and closed the door upon leaving, the sounds of the hall of curtains also faded away. Now, I could only hear my own beeps and the sound of the jet engine wrapped around my face. Plus, I now had a television. I could soothe myself with mindless reality shows and sports programming. It was heavenly.

Welcome to Hell, Comrade!

As night approached and I was still exhausted, I wish I could say I fell fast asleep. I wish I could say I slept soundly through the night. Instead, I found myself dreading bedtime. As someone who had not been two years old for some time now, it was a strange experience NOT to want to go to bed. Not only did I NOT want to go to bed, but I felt a bit panicked at the thought of closing my eyes and going to sleep. So much so that, despite my complete exhaustion, I stayed up late that night. Indeed, I felt panicked at the thought of going to bed well into my recovery time at home also. It was a helpless, almost childish feeling. I found it moderately embarrassing, especially when I got home, but in a place where you rely on the help of others for the most basic things in life, modesty and embarrassment fly quickly out the window.

I finally fell asleep. Of course, even if I had wanted to sleep through the night, that was not going to happen that night or any night during my entire stay in the hospital. It wasn't so much the sounds as it was the constant interruptions for blood pressure, finger pricks, x-rays, medicine, and shots in the stomach. It was always more challenging to get back to sleep after each interruption. Perhaps that was partly why I started to "wake up" much earlier than I usually do. That and the fact that the panicked feeling wasn't around when the sun was out.

I was ready for breakfast that next morning, but as I started eating it, I noticed something I had not noticed the night before. I looked out the window in my door and discovered that I was staring at the sealed entrance into the place where they take you to die. What was worse was that, at that moment, those sealed doors opened briefly, and I saw a stretcher being rolled in. It was an older man, and, like me, when I was wheeled through those doors, he was awake. I studied his face for the brief moment I could see him as he was wheeled past. He appeared to be quite old. The news had already been reporting that this disease was worse for the elderly. I wondered if he would soon be ventilated and if his family would soon be summoned to say goodbye. I started to pray for him and for his family. I prayed so fervently that I found my breakfast cold when I returned to eating. Even though I just woke up, I wanted to nap after that prayer. I would be very familiar with the constant feeling of exhaustion in the many months that followed. Of course, hadn't the Lord also said something about focusing on me? On saving my strength? But it's always the right thing to pray for others. Right?

Throughout that day, I saw others wheeled into where they take you to die. With each one, I found myself thinking, "Welcome to Hell, Comrade!" before I dismissed such thoughts from my head and started to offer up prayers for them. With each one, I felt a bit more exhausted. My doctor and respiratory nurse mentioned that my oxygen levels were not improving. They were not overly concerned at this point, but they had hoped I would start moving more in the right direction. In fact, I was moving a bit in the opposite direction. I didn't fully understand this at the time. I was still feeling much better than I had been before the firefighter hit me with that blessed O2 a few nights before. With a private room and television, I wasn't thinking about ventilators and sedation much anymore. Like a silly child, I thought they would release me to return home any time now.

I stayed up late again that night because I was just too afraid to go to sleep. But late-night programming becomes more mindless as the night wears on, even in the age of cable television and on-demand shows. I saw another comrade coming through the sealed doors as the night nurse entered the room for another shot in the stomach and a round of meds. After she left, I drifted off to sleep, having no idea I was meant to die that night.

Close Call

Before breakfast arrived that next morning, I was greeted by the concerned faces of a new doctor and my night nurse. It seems that the night nurse had been closely watching my oxygen levels through the night and had been feeding that information to the doctor on call. Unbeknownst to me, my oxygen levels had dropped sharply during the night. The doctor informed me that I was mere minutes away from the call to sedate and place me on a ventilator. It was a sobering punch in the gut. It scared me more than I had ever been scared in my life. No breakfast this morning because they were going to put me on my stomach in an attempt to get things moving back in the right direction. I had previously been told it was much better for my lungs to lie on my stomach, but watching football on a tiny television on your stomach is hard. A dumb decision on my part.

The doctor advised me they had spoken to my primary day-doctor in the ICU, and she had advocated for a wait-and-see approach overnight. She had informed them that, while my numbers may have gone down, I had a great attitude and a lot of spirit and that she would like to give me the opportunity to fight. The doctor said he was not entirely in agreement but deferred to the doctor who had spent more time with me. After the doctor left the room, the nurse got me flipped over on my stomach. I was scared but thankful for a second chance.

A few hours later, my primary ICU doctor came in to see me. With tears in my eyes, I thanked her. I thanked her for giving me a chance. I thanked her for not putting me on the ventilator. I thanked her for seeing me as a person with family and friends and much life yet to live, not just a patient with a critical oxygen level. She told me that this was it. This was my chance. I needed to lie on my stomach, use my "lung-stretching gizmo" (my words), and fight like heck. I was looking at a ventilator if my numbers did not improve by evening. I later learned that my doctor, Sarah (she was actually a physician's assistant, and that isn't her real name), had spoken to my wife several times and told her of my situation. People had been praying for me already, but I now know without a doubt that prayers through that night saved my life.

I found lying on my stomach strangely comforting (yet also uncomfortable). So much so that I drifted off to sleep. It was nearly lunchtime now. I was also removed from the lunch service while we focused on keeping me off the ventilator. It was good, though, as it gave me more time to get some much-needed sleep. Even more importantly, during that sleep, Jesus gave me a dream, showing me just what had taken place during the previous night.

Back From the Brink

I have never been much for dreams. In fact, when I do have dreams, I'm usually one of those weird lucid dreamers. I can control the action while dreaming. This isn't always the case, but it is my norm. That wasn't the case with this dream.

As I slept, I suddenly found myself in what I can only describe as a hellish place. I don't think it was actually hell, but it was the most miserable place I had ever seen. The ground was dry and charred. I didn't see any signs of vegetation. No signs of water. No trees or animals. Just barrenness. It felt hot. Even without signs of water around, it also felt humid. The air was stifling, even worse than the most hot and humid August day in the South.

Scattered about were what appeared to be something like bubbling lava pools. While I have never visited the geysers at Yellowstone, I have seen pictures, and these bubbling pools reminded me of the images I had seen. The sky was dark. If not for the bubbling lava pools, it would have been too dark to see much of anything. There were no people around. Just dryness, heat, darkness, bubbling pools, and a strong sense of death...perhaps my death.

As I surveyed this scene, suddenly, to my right, a man entered the frame. He was walking from my right to left, and I instantly knew he was Jesus. He walked with a purpose. He walked with authority. He didn't seem to even notice all the things in this scene that gave me pause and even abject fear. He just moved through silently at a peaceful, fast-walking sort of pace. He was in control, and whoever or whatever was lurking about in that place of death knew it.

He appeared to be carrying something under His arm. My eyes must be playing tricks because it looks like a person under his arm. He had them tucked in tight on His right hip, with his right arm around them. Like the way someone might playfully carry a child or perhaps a sack of potatoes. It's an effortless endeavor to Him even though the person is no child. In fact, they look like a full-grown man. As He turns ever so slightly, I can just see the side of his face a bit. I can just see the face of the man wrapped tightly under His arm. The man is...me.

I didn't ever get a good look at Jesus' face. Just a bit from the side. From the back. Later, when I was at home recovering, I relayed this story to my wife and two young children. They asked me what Jesus looked like. I couldn't really tell them. I just knew it was Him. They asked me to draw the scene I saw during that dream. I have never been very artistic, but I did my best. That not-very-artistic image can be seen with other pictures at www.backfromthebri nkbook.com.

I watched Jesus walk through the scene, carrying me under His arm. He exited the scene, and I woke up. Tears filled my eyes, and I found myself sobbing profusely. The sobbing was so intense that my oxygen level dropped slightly. I knew that would alert the nurse to check on me, so I had to gain control of myself a bit. I was able to slow the tears and control the sobbing just enough that nobody came to my room. Still, I was able to soak in that moment for a while. To soak in the deep, abiding love of Jesus. To somehow reconcile that I was meant to die that night. But for some undeserving reason, Jesus saved me Himself.

As I processed what I had seen, it became clear that Satan had meant to take my life that night. Whether I died in the night or was sedated and ventilated and slowly slipped away, he planned to take me out. I now became aware of why the Lord told me a few nights before to focus on myself and save my strength. He knew what was coming for me and just how much I would have to fight for my own life soon.

Jesus Himself had entered my spiritual world and brought me back from the brink of death. I was helpless, lying limp under His arm. I could do nothing on my own. I could not fight. I could not protect myself. I could not prevent Satan from carrying out his plan for me. I could not give back a husband to my wife. I could not guarantee that my children would have a father. I could not put my affairs in order or make a way for my family to return to a place where others could help them heal, live, and move on. The only thing there was in this place was Jesus.

I wasn't just given a second chance at life that night. I was also reminded of a valuable life lesson. We are nothing and have nothing and can do nothing apart from Jesus Christ. Any time we think we can care for ourselves or others. Any time we think we can make enough money or have enough power. Any time we feel that we have accomplished something. We should remember that we are simply wrong. Indeed, it is Jesus. Not us.

I felt humbled and shocked as I lay face down in that uncomfortable bed. I was humbled that Jesus would not only know who I was but also use some of His precious time to enter that place of death to carry me back to life personally. I was shocked because so many people on this earth are so much more deserving of this gift. I had "been a Christian" for most of my life. I attended Christian school and church. I had gone to Bible studies and even preached some. I had been a Christian most of my life and a "good person" as well, but I haven't lived my life for Jesus. I haven't surrendered myself to Him as King. I haven't bent the knee to Him as Lord. Indeed, my life to that point had been a self-centered patchwork of praying the prayers and going through the Christian motions. Why me?

I still don't know the answer to that question. I wish I could say that my life has been one of humble servitude to Jesus since that time. I wish I could say I had earned the gift that was given to me... a second chance. But I can't really say that. It has still been a daily grind, a daily struggle, like the life of any follower of Christ. Some days seem great, while others do not. And yet, by God's grace, I still have breath in my lungs and knowledge that has been seared into my foolish heart. I have a new testimony.

But the testimony only begins there. Yes, Jesus had brought me back from the brink, but it was only now that my fight would truly begin. Thankfully, God gave me many people to help along the way. Some prayed prayers.

Some gave medical care. But one kicked my butt. She was my angel of Blue.

Angel of Blue Part 1

Don't let anyone ever tell you that God doesn't have a sense of humor. Just look at a platypus or read about Balaam's talking donkey. For me, it was that my angel of Blue shared a name with...my ex-wife. Second, only to Jesus Himself, this angel truly saved my life. Awkward...

I met her on my first day in the private ICU room. She was my respiratory nurse. I had others but none quite like her. Eventually, she would become my only respiratory nurse. She was a traveling nurse from Florida, and I firmly believe God sent her to Texas just for me.

When she entered the room this time, I knew she meant business. I was still lying on my stomach, reeling a bit from my spiritual revelation, when I heard her unmistakable voice tell me that if I wanted to avoid the ventilator, I had best do what she said. There was no doubt about it; she had come to kick my butt.

My lungs were still very weak, and it was difficult to breathe most of the time, but she guided me back to life. Like a skilled race car driver, knowing the exact moment to let off the gas heading into a curve, she knew the exact point to which she could push me to get the desired result without pushing me too far. Her experience also told her that she needed to get me to commit fully, and she did that masterfully through prayer, encouragement, and an occasional expletive. This morning we were after enough progress to bring me back from the brink of a ventilator. Jesus had brought me back from the brink of death in the night. Now it was the job of my angel of Blue to bring me back from another brink.

She spent extra time with me that morning, and we got the job done...together. She left, knowing that we were back on the right track and that she had done her job that morning. When my P.A. Sarah came back later that afternoon, she told me with a tear in her eye that I was off the ventilator list...for now. We had dodged a bullet, and she felt confident that I was home free, but it was up to me to continue down the path to recovery. It was indeed my fight. She and others could only provide the tools and motivation, but I had to do the heavy lifting. I figured out a way to lie on my stomach, use my breathing gizmo, and watch sports on the television out of the side of my eye. Now that I was back on the meal list and they had specially ordered some food for me, I was back in Heaven.

"Movin' On Up!"

I had some fantastic medical providers during my time in the private ICU. One day my nurse from my first night in the hospital was caring for me. After checking on me, she wasn't quick to leave the room but usually hung around to chat for a few minutes. It was mostly pretty lonely in that room, and during this check-in, I asked her if she could stay longer. She said her other patients were pretty easy because they were sedated (hospital humor), so she had some extra time. She left for a few moments and brought back a chair into my room. She then spent the next two hours just talking with me about nothing and everything at the same time. I was away from family and friends and work and life, really. It was nice to have someone to talk with. To just be with. God made us to be social beings. With each birthday, I find that I like people less and less, but being completely without people can lead to insanity. Those two hours were the social shot I needed to keep going while I was housed in this place without the opportunity for visitors.

The night nurses were the best. I had two different male nurses, both with the same name. I will call them Chris and Christopher. Chris had been around for a while, and Christopher had only been a nurse for a few years. As the nights were less busy, especially in a place with mostly sedated patients, they would take the opportunity to stay and chat after they checked-in with me.

Christopher was prior military, and we had some intense conversations about politics and patriotism, and life in America. Since I spent most of my time alone in that room, mindlessly watching television, our conversations helped ensure my mind continued working. He had seen a lot during his time in the military, and just like painting calmed the combat demons for Bob Ross, Christopher found that helping others through nursing gave him a purpose and a means of keeping his own combat demons in check.

I found out that Chris was actually my neighbor. He lived just a few streets over from the house we were renting. Small world. I tried a few times to find his house after I got out but wasn't successful. I wanted to thank him in an environment that wasn't filled with beeping machines and facemasks. Those darn facemasks. I couldn't pick any of these medical saviors out of a line-up now if I had to. Just another unintended consequence of COVID-19.

When I say that these two men were the best, I mean it. They and so many others were the best because they went above and beyond all the time. Nobody ever just took my vitals, asked how I was doing, and then left. They would stay and chat for a minute even though I'm sure they were very busy. They would offer encouragement and even a needed hug. Chris actually fed me on several occasions when I was too weak to do it myself. He even shaved my face for me without hesitation when I asked. It had been a few days since I entered the hospital, and my short-cropped beard was getting long-cropped. It was pretty itchy with the jet engine around my face, and it was driving me crazy. Chris returned to the room with an electric razor and gave me a quick shave. I'm sure it wasn't the cleanest cut, but it did the trick. I was thankful for his willingness to DO the job of nursing and not just do a job. You can see a picture of his handiwork at www.backfrom thebrinkbook.com.

My time in the private ICU wasn't bad after Jesus brought me back from the brink, and I started fighting for my life. But I had been there a few days, and I desperately wanted to get out of the ICU. Now that the curtain was closed on my door window, I could only hear those sealed doors opening and shutting. Each time I wondered if somebody was arriving for work, coming to clean, or coming into the place they take you to die. Between that and the isolation in that small, cramped room, with nothing to look at on the walls, I was starting to feel a bit hopeless. I was improving physically, and I had fought enough to make the thought of a ventilator a distant memory, but

I needed to feel like I was really making progress. I needed to know that I was getting closer to going home. I had by now swallowed the bitter pill of realizing I wasn't getting out of here in a day or two. Nobody seemed to be able to give me a solid answer about how long I would be there. I was improving but nowhere near well enough to head home.

So, I'm not headed home yet, and I don't know for sure when I will be, but I would like a window that looks outside. I would like a room that isn't so cramped. I would like to be in a place that isn't sealed behind large metal doors, where incoming guests are already sedated or soon to be. I would like a nursing staff that doesn't mostly help unconscious patients. I feel like I'm dying up here, even though I'm farther away from death than when I entered. I desperately need to be in a place where I can have visitors. Please, God, help me!

Sarah entered the room. It would be the last time I would ever see her. We both teared up a little, but...I was movin' on up!

Angel of Blue Part 2

Sarah advised me I was moving on up, but in hospital time, that meant sometime in the next few hours...or days. Thankfully, it was the few hours variety, and I arrived in my new, larger, better-decorated room with a window in the place they take you to live. And who should be my first "visitor" at my new crib? Why, none other than my angel of Blue.

As it turned out, by the grace of God, she wasn't just a visitor. She had been transferred from the ICU starting the next day. She came to say "hi" and let me know our journey together was not over. She helped get me out of the ICU, and now she would help get me home. We teared up a little as we shared a moment only God could orchestrate. Understand that this hospital is enormous and easily employs hundreds of people. It has hundreds of rooms. The thought that we traveled together from the ICU to a regular room is genuinely astonishing. It was indeed a miracle.

I've Got Peace Like a...Pigeon?

I want to say that I went to bed quickly and slept like a baby that night, but that would not be true. I still had the panicked feeling when it was time to go to sleep. I still watched mindless television well into the night. I still woke up very early in the morning, not-so-refreshed from a few hours of something similar to sleep. And in that place, God provided a source of comfort. It was really a spectacle that first night, but it made the panicked feeling feel less panicky on subsequent nights.

Now that I had a window to the outside world, I wanted it to remain open. I couldn't say what floor I was on or what direction my window faced, but it didn't matter; it was far better than only seeing the next victim wheeled through the sealed metal doors. I couldn't see the sunset, but I could see glimpses of an orange and purple sky. Even as I basked in the beauty, I could feel the anxiety rising in my chest. I still feel it as I type these words all this time later. My mind was wandering a bit when I heard a thud on my window. What the what!?

I positioned myself to see the ledge just outside the window better, only to see a pigeon sitting on the ledge. Over the next few minutes, that one pigeon would become well over twenty pigeons. They were flying in and bedding down for the night, and it was quite a spectacle to watch. I had never really observed pigeon behavior before, but I can only describe this nighttime routine as chaos. I also better understood why calling someone a "pigeon brain" was not complimentary.

This was not a well-orchestrated transcontinental goose migration or the elegance of a hawk swooping down for a tasty meal. No, this was a hundred birds trying to occupy a space for twenty. Pigeons would fly in and crash into another pigeon. Sometimes a pigeon would fly in and land on another pigeon's head. They were bobbing their heads at one another in a bid for a small piece of the "ledge-bed." They were fluttering their wings at one another. This was no display of cooperation and sacrificial living. This was a raw version of "King of the Hill." You can see a few pictures of my new friends at www.backfromthebrinkb ook.com.

After the show was over, however, and the twenty or so survivors were nuzzling in for the night, there was a certain peace in watching their stillness and hearing the low hum of cooing. I found myself watching them for the next hour or so until the sun had dipped entirely behind the horizon, and darkness made it impossible to see outside. I could still hear the cooing, which was a much better sound than the television. I had muted it when I heard that first thud on the window. I now turned it off completely and just listened to the cooing outside my window. I turned off the lights, and as my eyes adjusted a bit, I could see their shapes against the window again. A nurse came in and asked if I wanted the window blind shut. I said to leave it open tonight. I didn't tell her that I wanted to just lay there and watch my new friends.

Bright New Day

I may have slept in a little that following day (meaning past my new waking hour of 5:00 am) because I was greeted by a light so blinding, I thought for a moment I had died in the night. I can see now why the nurse offered to close the blind the night before. Apparently, my room mainly faced to the east, and the sun was just rising in all its glory. It must have been time for the pigeons to start their day too, as one by one, they flew away to who knows where. This would become our daily routine. Just before bedtime, the pigeons would fly in and begin their nightly variety show on the window ledge. I would watch them and eventually find sleep to the sound of cooing. Then in a flash, they would fly away in the morning to start their day. I never saw one fly in during the day. As a matter of fact, I never saw a pigeon through my window during the day at all. But in the evening, it was like a whistle sounded somewhere to end their shift, and they would suddenly show up a hundred strong, vying for a spot on my ledge. Indeed, they were a source of great comfort during my time in that place. I was amazed at how God could accomplish so much through something so simple.

I missed Dr. Sarah from the ICU, but God provided a new, sensible doctor up there in the regular-person room. I met her that morning and was delighted to learn we were on the same page. Get me out of here. She said she would unleash my angel of Blue on me and push me to get off the jet engine oxygen pump and onto the much quieter oxygen machine. I could actually go home with a bit of oxygen still needed (and that is what happened), but she wanted to get me as close as possible to breathing on my own before I left. I was delighted to hear this plan, especially as I was starting to fear the thing that often keeps people in the hospital or even takes their life while there...catching something else. I wanted to Go Home!

Cast of Characters

Over the next several days, I had the privilege of having a few visitors. It was a bit surreal, to put it mildly, especially as I was only in my underwear. Unlike many people who spend time in a hospital bed (so I'm told), I never felt cold...ever. As a matter of fact, I had been burning up (I am naturally hot-natured anyway) since that first night in the ICU. This was much to the surprise of the nursing staff, who continually offered me extra hospital blankets. No, this sheet is just fine, thank you. So, instead of wearing a hospital gown and covering myself with multiple blankets, I spent my time under a sheet and in my underwear.

I had been instructed to sit up on the edge of the bed some during the day and not just lie in bed. I was doing just that, with my back to the door and my underwear barely covering important areas, when I got my first visitor. I heard the door open and caught a glimpse of someone entering the room out of the corner of my eye. I thought this doctor was dressed for the golf course, as they were wearing comfortable slacks and a golf shirt. As they came around into full view, I saw that it was instead my dean from my day job at the university. It was a pleasant and much-needed surprise. It had been several days since I had laid eyes on someone I knew. By this time, I was talking a lot on the phone with my wife and texting with her and a few others. I had even video-chatted with her and my kids a few times. But I had not seen a real live familiar face. I felt honored and blessed that he would take the time to come and see me. We visited for thirty minutes or so (they had visitors on a very short leash during COVID), and my spirits were certainly lifted for the remainder of that day.

My work partner and friend came to see me a few days later. This was a planned visit, but she, too, caught me in my underwear on the edge of the bed. Not one for always following silly rules, our visit went well past the one-hour limit and closer to three. That visit, too, lifted my spirits greatly. As a former law enforcement officer, I knew she had seen a lot, but I asked her if this was the first time she had ever had a lengthy conversation with her partner while they were clothed only in their underwear. She thought for a minute and, not surprisingly, said, "No." While in law enforcement, she had visited her then-partner in the hospital after he had a heart attack. Regardless, the shared law enforcement history took the awkwardness out of the scene. She told me she had deferred to my dean for a visit a few days earlier. That's the kind of humble, sacrificial person she is. I was thankful for both visits. I needed them. But the best was yet to come.

The next day I was to receive a visit from my wife. She had arranged for someone from my job to watch the kids (the hospital was not allowing anyone under 18 to visit), and she was coming up to see me. I couldn't wait. Visiting each other while she was wearing the space suit was strange. She was fully gowned, and I could only make out her eyes through the mask and face shield she was required to wear. Due to COVID, this was all I had seen of anybody since arriving. Hospital staff had to change gowns, masks, and gloves between each visit and between patients. I can't even imagine the waste generated by this exercise, not to mention the cost. When I first entered the ICU, I saw stacks and stacks of boxes. Only later was I informed that those boxes contained Personal Protective Equipment (PPE). Hospitals were going through a lot in those days.

Even though I couldn't really see my wife's beautiful face, I was delighted that she was there. We visited for a couple of hours, talking about everything and nothing. She told me of all the people praying for me. Apparently, the small prayer circle had morphed into something quite large. I learned that people from throughout the country were praying for me, many of them I did not even know. I learned that my mother-in-law felt compelled to be anointed with oil and prayed over on my behalf. While I knew that people had been praying, it became ever so clear during our time together just how much was happening spiritually on my behalf. It was pretty humbling, really. Who am I? My eyes filled with tears as I learned that the anointing and prayers spearheaded by my mother-in-law directly coincided with the night Jesus brought me back from the brink. I'm so thankful she listened to God's still, small voice compelling her to act. It saved my life.

Our visit seemed to end before it started. She had overstayed the silly rules a bit, and my nurse could only let the rules bend for so long. Besides, the kids were probably asking when their mom was returning. My wife had removed her protective glove while we were together and placed her hand, skin on skin, against mine while we talked. Before leaving, she removed her face shield, pulled down her mask, and ventured a kiss. I was a bit hesitant at first due to the whole COVID thing. She said she had it already and wasn't worried. It was a kiss second only to our first. I teared up as she left. They were tears of joy at still being alive to kiss her lips and tears of sadness that I couldn't leave this place with her that day. When was I getting out of here?

Between those visits, I also had the absolute privilege of meeting so many wonderful people. From the people bringing my meals or taking out the trash to nurses and doctors, the staff at this place was top-notch.

One nurse was from Slovakia. She had come to America many years back with her family when she was much younger. She only had a slight accent. Asking about it is how we got not only to a bit of her history but also a history lesson on the splitting of the former Czechoslovakia into two nations and that one of them (The Czech Republic) was soon to change its name again. She had an infectious joy about her. For someone who had seen and known what it was like not to be free, she was thankful for her freedom in this country. She also feared that we were walking down a path toward giving it all away.

I also had a nurse who was actually a doctor. This was something she did not tell the others. She was from Florida and had a Doctor of Nursing Practice (DPN). She ran a medical office and had taken some time off to help in the fight against COVID as a traveling nurse. She felt like the other nurses would treat her differently if they knew she was a DPN, so she swore me to secrecy. She also had a holistic approach to medicine. While she obediently followed my doctor's orders for my care, she was also fond of the healing properties of hot lemon tea. This became a nightly routine for us. I grew to request the hot tea, and she always obliged. She would typically sit with me and talk a bit while I drank it.

I met a variety of veteran medical providers, as well as newbies. I even had a few nursing students. At my expense, one got to experience giving a shot to a real patient for the first time. Still living the healing power of fruit (physically but even more spiritually), I eagerly agreed to let her give it a shot...and me one too. Now, understand that I'm not too fond of needles. Actually, I don't like them at all. For much of my life, I had dreaded the idea of being in the hospital and having to endure IVs and shots. Now, here I was with 2 IVs (3 attempts), finger pricks multiple times per day, shots in the stomach multiple times daily, and several blood draws from my wrist area. I had become a pro in a sport I never wanted to play.

Her first attempt on a real patient was...well...an attempt. It was a far cry from some of the veteran sticks I had gotten since my arrival, but I praised her for it anyway. I had brought the deep spiritual understanding of the power found in the Fruit of the Spirit with me from the ICU. Just like in that place, it was also noticed and welcomed up here. I later learned I had achieved "favorite patient" status up here too. Every nurse wanted me as a patient because I was nice, thankful, and low maintenance. It wasn't much. Nobody was "getting saved," to my knowledge. But hopefully, some seeds were sown that might grow into a spiritual harvest one day. That seems to be the way God works.

Indeed, the medical staff here was top-notch. I cannot say enough good things about the people I encountered here. Aside from the one blunt nurse during my arrival in the ER, every other person I met here was friendly, helpful, understanding, and eager. Not long before I left, I learned just why.

Right Place, Right Time Part 2

Before God spoke our universe into existence, He knew COVID-19 would be perpetrated on the world. He knew that the devil would attempt to use it to take my life. And He put measures in place all those many millennia ago to "stack the deck" in my favor. I had already recognized that coming to Texas was a Godsend for reasons other than I initially thought. Being in this state was indeed the right place at the right time. But it went even deeper than that.

I asked the veteran "hot tea" nurse just a day or so before I left why everyone here seemed so eager to help. Why everyone had a smile on their face and seemed truly interested in not just my health but in...me. "Because this hospital is a Level 1 Trauma Teaching Hospital", she said. "This is the best of the best." She told me they can do pretty much anything here. They can handle any trauma. They have doctors for just about any ailment. But most importantly, this is a teaching hospital. This is where people come to learn how to be the best. They are eager because they want to learn. They aren't jaded yet. They still truly care. The smiles are genuine. The concern is real. The eagerness isn't faked. This is why I had a mixture of newbies and veterans. This is why the newbies were learning from the veterans. This is why I had the occasional student and even got the inaugural needle stick from one. Now it made sense.

After she left the room and I thought more about what she said, I was in awe of the goodness of God. The Bible tells us that His ways are not ours. It tells us that He loves us and cares for us. But our understanding of these things is so very limited. We know His love is largely expressed in that He sent His only Son to die on the cross in our place.

But we miss so much of the daily, minute-by-minute love He demonstrates for us.

I thought of one such time that happened to my wife early in our marriage. She was invited to go somewhere with a group of ladies from the church. She had planned to go but bowed out at the last moment. Within 15 minutes of the time, they were originally supposed to pick her up, they were involved in a car wreck, and one lady died. We grieved for that woman and her family but praised God that my wife didn't feel right about going that day. God saved her in that moment. He had planned it even before He put Adam and Eve in the Garden or called Moses from the burning bush. His love is so rich, and His ways are so mysterious.

Indeed, God had put us in the right place at the right time by taking us to Texas. We didn't know it when we arrived, and at times we thought going there was not of God. But we had been in town less than three months when this ordeal started. Thank God for Texas! But even more, God brought me to a place with the best possible medical care when I needed it. God works miracles in many ways. Sometimes He heals someone of some malady outright. Other times He works miraculously to heal them through doctors and nurses. The biggest miracle for me is that He set this all up even before time as we know it began. That is an all-powerful, all-knowing, all-present God. That is a God who put me in the right place at the right time...twice.

"Movin' Out"

It was a welcome change to move from the constant sound of the jet engine to the near silence of the nasal cannula. I had been attached to it for so long that it was a bit eerie when they removed it. But it wasn't just the silence that was welcome. That thing was rather unwieldy. If you can imagine trying to move around in bed and do the daily chores of life while wearing SCUBA gear, you can start to get the picture. I had much more freedom of movement now, both in moving around in the bed and in the distance from the bed. My lungs had been catching up with my desire to leave, and it was nice to move about the room...albeit with a 30-foot air hose still attached.

I had no concerns now about a ventilator. I knew I wouldn't die here...at least from COVID. I was going home sometime. But as the days started to wear on, I became increasingly concerned about developing another issue while in the hospital. It seems that too often, a person goes into the hospital for one thing and gets sick or even dies from some other issue that developed while there. Constantly lying in a bed and being pumped full of a cocktail of drugs is hard on a person. The longer one is there, the greater the risk of an error. I was getting several shots daily in my stomach to ward off blood clots, but there was no guarantee. I had known of people who went into the hospital for one thing, started getting better, and then got much worse because of some other thing. The more I thought of this possibility, the angrier I got. I was going to be ticked if I survived COVID only to die of something else I got while here. Each time the doctor came in to check on me, I expected to hear some bad news that would necessitate an even longer stay and additional treatments. I wanted out of here.

Of course, if you think about that fear, it was really ridiculous. Jesus Himself had brought me back from the brink of death. He had thwarted the plan the devil had for my demise. He had shown it all to me, so I knew it was Him. So that I knew it was His gift to me, my wife, and my children. And now, here I was, afraid I might get something else and die in this place. Oh, ye of little faith.

I had met some amazing people in this place. I am actually still friends with my angel of Blue. Strangely, I felt that I didn't want to leave them. They were a source of comfort, I suppose. They had become my caretakers. As much as I wanted to go, I feared not having them and this place to support me after I got home. In many ways, this adventure would be over. I would be back at home, back to everyday life. To be sure, I would have a long recovery ahead of me, but this wild adventure would be over...at least this first part. I couldn't wait to see my family. But I was afraid too. Afraid not just from the lingering issues with my breathing but also because I had changed while in the hospital. Every dad wants to be strong for his kids, but I was coming home weak and needy. After arriving home, I wasn't as grumpy for a while. It was like one person left in the ambulance, perhaps never to return, and another was coming home.

I was elated when the doctor told me I was headed home the next day. I would be leaving still on oxygen, but my level had gone from the jet engine to a 1 or 2. I didn't know what that meant but was told it was good enough to go home. I had to take oxygen equipment home, and it would become another close friend for a few weeks. The sound of the machine filled our house day and night. A constant reminder that I had come home a shell of what I was but that I had indeed come home.

The next day arrived, and I was chomping at the bit to leave. I was told I had to get one final check from the doctor...a different doctor. I immediately started to panic. The other doctor was sensible and willing to take a risk or two. They were sending me home in less-than-ideal circumstances but with my assurance that I would follow their orders and take it easy, they had agreed to let me go.

Would this new doctor agree with that plan? Would they want to change things up? Would they want to keep me in this place longer? Thankfully, the new doctor was on board with the plan. I was going home...or so I thought.

As the hours wore on, from morning into lunchtime, I started to worry that something had changed. Maybe it was the morning x-ray of my lungs. Perhaps something turned up in my most recent blood draw. What could be taking so long? I had asked my nurse to tell me when to let my wife know I was ready to leave. It was a 20+ minute drive to the hospital from our house, and I wanted to work out the timing as best as possible. The nurse said to call my wife to come pick me up. It was time. I had changed into regular clothes and sat on the side of the bed, waiting for my ride down to the front door. Had they forgotten me?

As it turns out, they had forgotten me. Somebody forgot me. I'm not sure who. The oxygen people were supposed to bring up the equipment I would be taking home, and someone was supposed to come up to transport me down to where I would be picked up. I sat for what seemed like three hours. Probably because it was about three hours. My wife and kids had been waiting in the car. We had been texting, but I had no idea what was happening. My nurse suddenly came into the room, not expecting to see me. She said, "Are you still here?" I thankfully held my tongue, but in my head, I thought, "Well, I'm sitting here, aren't I?" She couldn't believe it and said she would be right back. After some phone calls, things started moving. The oxygen people did their thing, and the nurse returned with a wheelchair. She would wheel me down herself. But before we got that far, the transport technician entered the room. They had been busy with a line of people ahead of me. No matter. Let's get me loaded and out of here.

I thanked those I passed as I was wheeled by the nurse's station. I didn't know if they had all cared for me in some way or not. I didn't care. They were to be thanked for the sacrifices they made for me and for those they will make for others. They were on the front line in the COVID fight and standing in the gap the rest of the time. They don't get enough credit. I thanked them all again and again. Before hitting the elevator, there was one last piece of business. They had set up a bell to ring for those who had survived COVID. I rang it with all my heart (you can see that picture too at www.backfromthebrinkbook.com). I had survived, not on my own but with the Godly help of top-quality medical staff and a direct spiritual intervention from Jesus. I had survived. My wife would still have a husband. My kids would still have a father. I would still be among the living. COVID didn't get me. I had survived. Now...let's go home.

Recovery

I do the lion's share of the driving in our family, so it was humbling to not only surrender the wheel to my wife but, in fact, to ride in the back. The front passenger seat of our van would not accommodate my travel oxygen tank. No matter. I was headed home, and I couldn't be happier. Things were certainly looking up. I had survived COVID. I had survived the hospital. My oxygen machine was a solid 2 (I still didn't know what that meant, but only that I needed to get to a "0"). It was only up (or down) from here.

Sadly, things came crashing down those first few days back. I can't say exactly what it was. Perhaps this was just normal. Nevertheless, I had to dial the oxygen back up to about a 4, and I lay on the couch feeling nearly the same as before I left that same couch 11 days earlier. It wasn't COVID again. According to some science, I would now have a near super-immunity to COVID for some time. No, maybe it was just exhaustion...physical, mental, and emotional. It was Halloween, and I was going to the "party" as an invalid.

While in Texas, we learned that they do everything big in Texas...including Halloween. Due to my condition, my wife had already decided that having Halloween inside our house would be wise. My kids were never much for traditional trick-or-treating anyway, but as they saw the celebration unfolding out our front window, they couldn't help but go outside at least to watch. Our neighborhood was a large one filled with upper-middle-class cookie-cutter homes. The perfect neighborhood for trick-or-treating. The street outside was filled with people and cars. We had left our lights off, so nobody came to our house. Still, the Halloween vibe swept into our home too. Looking outside, my wife and kids even saw someone on stilts walking down the street. It was quite the celebration that I enjoyed the next day through the pictures my wife had snapped.

Inside our home, the celebration was kicking off too. My wife had devised a trick-or-treating route for my kids to navigate up and down the stairs between the two of us. I was downstairs with a bowl of candy sitting beside me, and she took the upstairs post. The kids didn't take long to fill their buckets with candy, but the celebration didn't end there. The kids took it upon themselves to use dress-up clothes to fashion other costumes. Over the next few hours, they put together several very clever Halloween costumes. I can't say I thoroughly enjoyed the festivities that evening, but we had some laughs a few days later when I was feeling better and could look through the pictures.

Still, even in my condition, my wife and I got into the action. My daughter had dressed my wife as a "rich lady." She sat next to me for a picture, which I entitled "The invalid and the gold-digger." You can enjoy it along with other pictures from this journey at www.backfromtheb rinkbook.com. Even though I was starting to think I had left the hospital too soon, it turned out to be one of the best Halloweens ever.

As bedtime approached, I started to feel the fear creeping in that I felt each night at the hospital. It was made worse because I had gone downhill after getting home. It was my second night home, and I was delighted to sleep in my own bed, but I still felt panicked. It was irrational, yes. Believe me, I prayed and prayed about it. But the fear was still there. It wasn't that my prayers fell short or that God didn't hear them. Sometimes, God lets us go through challenging situations simply because it's good for us. We may flail around, gripe about it, and even get upset with Him sometimes, but He stays the course in those places because He loves us. He can see what lies ahead and the growth we will have in those places. He truly wants the best for us even when we would rather avoid the path altogether.

I think I slept that night, but I'm not sure. I wasn't sure the previous night either. Regardless, I had awoken early...very early...each morning. I did this in the hospital, and it was to continue during my recovery at home. However, I can't say my wife was keen on this part of the new me. I wasn't an early riser before I went into the hospital, so this 5 am thing was out of the norm. This was especially so, as I also had developed quite an appetite while in the hospital. This seemed counterintuitive for a hospital stay, and I certainly didn't gain weight in the hospital (I had lost quite a few pounds, as it seems most people do), but I did eat almost every bite of every meal while there. Before the hospital, I usually just ate some type of fiber bar for breakfast. Now, I was into eggs, bacon, and my favorite with every meal...fruit. My wife sensed my waking movements and rolled over to catch eyes with me. "You're ready for breakfast, aren't you?" Yes, I am.

Each day I would station myself on the couch. I also had a rolling office chair nearby that I would switch to as needed. I did a lot of sitting in those early days, so I needed options to keep my backside from hurting. After a few days, I got my oxygen level back to 2. Things were headed in the right direction again, but it was still hard. Walking from the bedroom to the living room or the living room to the bathroom was difficult. The walking wasn't the hard part. It was the breathing. In the early days, I would have to sit for a minute or so to get my breathing back to a normal level again. After my experience, I feel for people who have asthma. On many occasions, I felt like I would die after the short walk to the bathroom. My breathing was so shallow, and I couldn't seem to catch my breath after so much "physical exertion." It's a scary feeling. Usually, my wife would have to calm me down, sometimes just holding me in her arms until my breathing slowed. While I like being comforted as much as the next person, it's difficult as a man to feel helpless. And I felt helpless.

I was so helpless that I didn't have the energy to wash my own hands after using the bathroom. The walk to the bathroom and the walk back that I knew was shortly coming just took everything out of me. I would just sit on the toilet (clothed, lid down) and hang my hands over the sink. My wife would gently wash and dry them for me. It was comforting and humbling at the same time. It became our routine for the days and weeks to come. Over time, I became less dependent on her help in the bathroom. In the early days, I had her stand there with me before washing my hands. I just didn't want to be alone, I guess, even in that place. I was a bit afraid to be alone. But things were getting back to normal a bit more each day.

After a week or so, my wife started really encouraging me to get up and move more. I knew I should, but the fear of being unable to catch my breath made for a convenient crutch. I just wasn't ready for that. Still, I yielded and started taking short walks around the living room. It wasn't much, but it gave me a sense of accomplishment and made her happy. She didn't give up and finally convinced me to go sit outside on the covered back porch. By this point, I was off the oxygen completely, but we had the machine running in case I needed it in an emergency. I thought this would probably be just that emergency, so to be safe I put the oxygen on. I was glad that I made it out back and into a chair without incident. The sun and fresh air certainly did me some good.

For several weeks after arriving home, I needed a lot of help bathing. My wife, as usual, was right there to help. Indeed, this entire season in our lives was good for both of us. It was hard, to be sure, but it deepened our bond with one another. I played the part of the helpless person, and she played the part of the caretaker. We never saw this coming and certainly didn't ask for it, but it is a time we will always remember with both fondness and sadness. On this day, however, it was a personal milestone for me. My wife woke up to me walking out of the bathroom. My hair was wet, and I was fully clothed for the day. With great surprise, she said, "Did you shower!?" Yes, I did, and I did it all by myself. The smallest things can be considered a great triumph when you're in the desert, even though they might sound silly to others.

There was no denying now that I was on my way back. I went to the doctor for a check and got a note saying I was fit for light duty. Thankfully, my work allowed me to go to light duty status, working from home. It gave me a little something to do other than watching television. I could go to the bathroom by myself and wash my hands. Yay me! I was walking all around the house without the need for supplemental oxygen. Actually, we had already returned the oxygen equipment (talk about burning the ships). I could go sit out back all by myself. Obviously, I was ready to mow the grass.

Ok, I wasn't quite ready to mow the entire yard by myself. For some obsessive reason, I thought a lot about the grass while in the hospital and after coming home. I planned to mow it right before I got sick, so it had gotten higher than I liked. This was such an obsession for me that I asked about the grass during my first telephone conversation with my wife while I was in the ICU. My wife ended up mowing it (bless her heart). She did this even as she herself was feeling the effects of COVID (yes, my whole family got it in the beginning, too. Thankfully, I was the only one who had so much trouble). I suppose I wasn't in my right mind to "demand" such a thing, but she was a real trooper. But now I was home, and as a man, I needed to get back to being a man. My breathing was good, not great, at this point. Still, I had overcome before, and I needed to overcome now. Well, I did overcome...about a third of the yard.

I started to feel winded and went to sit in a folding chair in the garage. One of my kids happened to come out, and I said to get Mom. Naturally, with all that we had just been through, she thought the worst and came quickly into the garage. I suppose she expected to see me lying on the ground gasping for air. Finding me sitting in a chair with the sheepish, childish look of "yeah, I know, you told me" on my face, she took a video of me instead (there is a still shot at www.backfromthebrinkbook.com). We still get a good laugh out of that video. I look like a kid caught with his hand in the cookie jar. Plus, she now had to finish up the grass, which was not in her plan for the day. Sorry, honey.

Even though my first lawn experience was a bust, I was still well down the road to recovery. Christmas break was quickly approaching, and we planned a trip to visit family in Tennessee and Georgia on our way to Christmas in Michigan's Upper Peninsula. It would be a big test. I may be on the road to full recovery, but was I up for the test? By this point, I had attended an end-of-year event at work without incident, so I was feeling confident. I had started doing the driving around town again, but was I up for hours behind the wheel?

We closed up our house for the next month and hit the road. I had not seen any family besides my wife and two younger kids since going to the hospital. The reunions were tearful and thankful. It was something we all needed. I did all the driving on this trip, and it wasn't a struggle. I was getting back to my old self day by day. I had survived COVID. I was even starting to be grumpy again.

Epilogue

During this trip, my wife and I independently came to the same conclusion. We were too far away from the help and support of family during this ordeal. While being wheeled into the ambulance, I was thinking about how in the world my family would get back to our primary residence in Michigan if I didn't make it out of this alive. I learned later that my wife was thinking the same thing at precisely the same moment. We were over 1,000 miles away, with a house full of stuff, a lease agreement that didn't expire until the following May, and not one but two cars. I can't begin to imagine the logistical nightmare this would have been while simultaneously mourning my passing (not to mention the logistical nightmare of getting my body to wherever it would be buried). We had gone west and were in just about the best possible place for my ordeal in the hospital, but we needed to be closer to family.

With much prayer and discussion, we decided to leave Texas and head back east. Thankfully, the Lord provided employment for me in a place nearly equidistant between my family and my wife's family. Ironically, this is almost precisely where we tried to move when we left Tennessee five years earlier. Our plan then was to be equidistant, but it didn't quite work out. We had a deal to buy a house that fell through, and we decided just to continue north to the area of my wife's family. We spent over two years there before our move to Nebraska. We don't always understand the Lord's timing in things (I still don't with this one), but here we are, about five hours from my wife's family and our primary residence and about seven hours from our family in Tennessee. Things seem to be working for this season of our lives.

I started thinking about this story after my recovery and Christmas break family visits. As I told and re-told this story to different family members, several of them said I should write it down. I would like to say that I started on it immediately, yet here we are, nearly two years later, when people have mostly forgotten about COVID, and some only say the word COVID through clenched teeth. But

I set out to write this story, and that's what I have done. What will happen with it from here is totally in God's hands.

Some people ask if I have what they call "long COVID." I'm not sure I know exactly what that means. I'm equally not sure that the folks in the medical field do either. There is still much confusion and many shell games being played with the whole COVID Pandemic thing. Still, even without a diagnosis, I think there are some lingering effects for me. The one thing I'm really aware of is my breathing. My oxygen level is routinely at 98-99 percent now, but I still get winded more quickly than I did before. One reason for that might be that I'm out of shape. I will own that one. But it just seems different to me. My job would not be considered "active" compared to many others, but I do spend a lot of time each week on my feet. So, my life isn't sedentary. Yet, it doesn't seem that I can boost my cardio much. Maybe I'm just not trying hard enough. Who knows? Nonetheless, I'm at present blaming it on having this COVID experience. Hopefully, it will improve over time (assuming I up my cardio game too).

We certainly don't live each day thinking about this experience now, but it is always with us. Sometimes one of us will share a humorous memory from this time and laugh. Occasionally someone will voice the fear they had then and the joy that I'm still around. It's like any other trauma, I suppose. Once the waters have stilled, your life no longer revolves around it. But it has become a part of the fabric of your life. It isn't just one of those things you remember, like a childhood birthday party or a favorite moment with a grandparent. Those fond memories you can access anytime but don't necessarily alter your life. They don't become a part of your DNA. Trauma is different. Whether it's a divorce, the loss of a dear one, losing everything, or even almost dying of COVID, it becomes part of your physiology. Part of your psychology. Even when you are not consciously aware, it is still silently directing your life in some way. You find tightness in your chest suddenly and don't quite know from whence it came. You make small and even life-altering decisions, and your trauma has a seat at the table for those decisions.

That is what this COVID survival story is for us, and yet it doesn't always drive our lives toward glory, so to speak. The spiritual aspect alone should have me spreading the gospel of my "new testimony" to anyone who will listen and even those who won't. I wish I could say that was the case, but it is not. In many ways, normal life has crept back in and reclaimed the driver's seat. I am getting grumpier with each passing year of life. I find myself concerned about the direction of our country and the world. I feel hopeless sometimes thinking about what will be left for my children and grandchildren. I falter daily in my Christian walk and spend more time feeling like I am displeasing God instead of earning and owning this gift He has bestowed upon me. That's the crazy thing about life. A loved one dies, and we move on. We get divorced, and we move on. We lose a job or business, and we move on. We have a near-death experience, and we move on. God does something amazing and miraculous in our life...and we move on. Don't believe me? Just look at the Israelites in the Old Testament. How many times did God do something amazing and miraculous for them, and they moved on...often to idolatry? We are so silly, and yet God loves us so dearly. We have moved on, but we haven't forgotten. Now, maybe we can begin to tell the story. Perhaps the story will cause another person to open their heart to Jesus. And isn't that what the trauma is really about for a believer?

Lessons Learned

I started this story with my "boring, old testimony." The first lesson to learn from this experience is simply that there is no such thing. The power of the Cross to save a lost soul is all the testimony you need, and regardless of whether that soul was saved from a life of drug addiction or saved from a life growing up in the church doesn't matter. In short, there is no such thing as a "boring, old testimony." I wish I had fully realized this before. Perhaps I would not have spent most of my life using this Christian myth as a crutch for not spreading the gospel message to those around me. Indeed, we are so weak and foolish.

Our testimony doesn't begin and end with our salvation experience. In fact, it follows us throughout our life and changes over time. When the preacher says evangelism is simply sharing what Jesus did for us, it seems we think they mean our salvation experience only. Perhaps the confusion is in the wording. It's not what Jesus did for us but what He has done over time for us, what He is currently doing in our lives, and what He will do for us in the future. If I stop at my salvation experience, it really can sound boring. I grew up in church and Christian schools. One day I got saved like every other kid in those circumstances. That's what Jesus did for me. Boring.

To begin, the salvation experience is so much more than that. Before I even existed, Jesus knew me and loved me. Indeed, He was thinking of me while He hung on the Cross. The blood He spilled on that hill washed away MY sins. When He rose from the dead, He thought about how that act would pave the way for eternal salvation for ME.

When you really think about it, the circumstances of your life when you accept His call don't even come up.

Then add to all that the idea that perhaps it is harder to call someone to a truly committed life as a Christ follower from...out of the church. Wait a second, you say! That can't be! It's a difficult pill to swallow but stay with me. Growing up in church and Christian schools, I learned Bible characters and stories. I learned spiritual concepts and principles. I learned Christian doctrine and all about Jesus dying for my sins. I learned all of the stuff and tearfully accepted Jesus as my Savior...twice. But did my life really show all of that afterward? Has my life been one of a faithful follower of Jesus Christ?

The church in the United States has existed in freedom since our founding. Indeed, much of our nation's history is about those seeking religious freedom. We are thankful that we have not known persecution and adversity. But it is in the cauldron of persecution and adversity that much spiritual growth and advancement takes place. This leaves many of us church folk with a solid doctrine that doesn't translate well into holy living. We look like the world, and non-believers see it. We stay silent as the things of God are pitched to the curb. We attend church on Sunday and feel righteous while we look on as those around us suffer and even fall into eternal damnation. We have spent a lot of time on autopilot. It can be difficult to go from lost to a true Christ follower for all of those reasons and more. Maybe a "Christian" but not a true follower of Jesus Christ. So, don't discount the power it takes to save a soul out of the church.

But we would be unwise to stop with what Jesus did for us in our salvation experience. Think about all He has done for you since then and share that with the people around you. Yes, He died on the Cross for you, but He also healed you of cancer, brought your prodigal son or daughter back, provided your next meal after you lost your job during the pandemic, blessed your gently-loved clothing ministry to the poor, and on and on and on. A preacher once suggested that we start and keep a list of all these things. On days when you are feeling down. During times of famine and desert in your life. When you feel hopeless, read through that list and remember truly ALL that Jesus has done for you. It might be pretty shocking. Those are things God has done in your life. That is YOUR testimony.

And don't forget what He will do for you. That, too, is part of your testimony. That is where you can talk about no more tears being shed to those who are crying, food aplenty to those who are hungry, and a mansion to those who are homeless. Because the message of salvation is not just about being saved from sins. It is not just escaping the eternal damnation of hell. It is not even just the concept of an eternal existence in some magical place we call Heaven. Instead, it is the fact that in this place called Heaven, we have no more fear. No more want. No more pain and suffering. No more trials and tribulations. No more hunger. No more tears. No more...broken world. It is simply...Perfect. And who wouldn't want that?

Another lesson I learned from this experience was just how much power there is in the Fruit of the Spirit. I've heard many sermons on the Fruit of the Spirit from Galatians. At Christian school, I memorized the passage from Chapter 5 many times. Like many Christians, I suspect, I always thought, "Yeah, got it, I need to be nice and love others and...gulp...even be patient and so forth." But I never really considered the power of the Fruit or why they're called Fruit in the first place.

The point of the list in Galatians is not to give one a list of things to do. Frankly, the more I've tried to be patient, the less patience I've had. The more I've tried to have peace, the less I've known. The more I've wanted to love, the less lovable I've felt. These are not things to try at all. Don't get me wrong, we should seek to be these things, but when it comes to the true meaning of this passage, we have the cart before the horse.

A fruit tree produces fruit, but the tree was there before the fruit. The fruit is a by-product of something else. It is a sign that the tree is healthy and doing what a fruit tree is supposed to do. Likewise, for a Christ follower, the Fruit of the Spirit in one's life is a sign that they are healthy spiritually and doing what they're supposed to be doing. In other words, we need not put so much effort into trying to have fruit. Instead, we simply need to follow Christ. By doing that, we will be healthy spiritually. We will do what we're supposed to do. And by extension, the sweet taste of the Fruit of the Spirit will spill over from our lives into the lives of the people around us.

I would like to think that, during my hospital stay, the Fruit spilled over out of my life because of my spiritual health and because I am doing what I'm supposed to be doing. I wish that were the case, but the Lord knows I'm a mess. Instead, I believe the Lord gave me a window into what the world around me would look like if my life did produce such Fruit. I felt like a new person after getting hit with that sweet, pure oxygen. It brought me back to life, so to speak, and that feeling of life produced joy, peace, love, and so on. God was letting me see what my life could look like and how it could impact the people around me.

Even in the secular world, we're told that a smile can change things. A hug can alter the course of someone's day.

I've seen people wearing t-shirts that simply say, "Be Nice." If those things can change someone's day, imagine how "being nice" to someone while infused with the power of the Fruit of the Spirit can change their life. The Lord let me see a bit of that firsthand. I got to see how it put a smile on another's face (well, I had to see it in their eyes and voice in this context...you know, the mask thing). I saw how it put a spring in their step. It made them want to do a better job. They passed it on to others. And in the confines of a "short" 11-day hospital stay, I came to be known as the best patient in the ICU and on the regular hospital floor. Granted, I had no personal knowledge of my competition at that time, but I would like to think that it was the Fruit at work in my life. And just think of the power of those same Fruit of the Spirit when you live a life wholly sacrificed to Jesus Christ. It may just go beyond putting a smile on someone's face...it may literally save their life.

I also learned a moderately uncomfortable and confusing lesson about what we might term "self-care" today. At the moment, it felt more like being selfish, and as all of us Christians know, that is not Godly. So, what gives? Well, to start with, I do think that our modern idea of self-care can be selfish. There is nothing wrong with ensuring we are our best physically, mentally, and emotionally. But, as with all of life, those things are rooted in our relationship with God. If we try to care for ourselves just for the sake of caring for ourselves, we will miss the point entirely. Instead, caring for ourselves under the guidance and direction of God, and the physical, mental, and emotional taking a back seat to the spiritual, will we only then be on the right track. As the Fruit of the Spirit is a sign of what lies beneath, genuinely caring for ourselves is a by-product of our commitment to following Christ. It is a sacrifice of praise and not a selfish endeavor.

Regardless, at that moment, I couldn't believe God would direct me to stop praying for the people around me and conserve my energy for myself. Yet, I learned a bit about prayer and was reminded that God's ways are not like ours. We tend to think of prayer as only working in the moment. As we are bound by time and live linear lives, that makes sense to us. But God is timeless and exists in all times at all times. Prayers can be stored up. They can collect in a large bucket, if you will, and maybe even be used for something different than you intended. Wait, what!? We think it is our prayers that make things happen. It is not. The power of God is what makes things happen. Prayer is simply an act of obedience, a sign that we are aligned with God and with that power. In other words, your prayers do not make God more powerful. He has all the power already. He actually doesn't need them. But He wants them more for us than for Him. They are an opportunity for us to align ourselves with Him. He already knows what we want and need and what's best for us and for others. Why pray, then? Because through prayer, we are closer to Him.

So, other people were also praying for my comrades in the ICU. Other people had prayed for them over the years. People had perhaps prayed for them even before they were born. The angels themselves had offered and were now offering prayers for them. My prayers added to the bucket, but God was simply telling me that He had it under control. He didn't need more prayers at that moment. He needed me to save my energy to prepare myself to fight for my own life. It still seems a bit strange and mildly (now) uncomfortable for me to consider. It strikes against so much doctrine that I have learned over the years. Perhaps so much of our doctrine isn't actually God's way of doing things.

I also learned from this "adventure" that God still does miracles today. I've heard some Christians say that miracles were used during Jesus' time to get the church up and going. Now we have good solid doctrine and a strong evangelistic message, so we don't really need miracles anymore...at least not in the American church. It seems to me that miracles do still happen in other countries. Of course, this all really depends on one's definition of a miracle. Still, miracles do happen daily in the lives of all sorts of people in every part of the globe. God is indeed at work in people's lives through doctrine and an evangelistic message and, yes, through miracles. He did a miracle in my life.

Many people survived COVID. Many people left the hospital after being admitted with COVID. Many people spent much more time in the hospital with COVID than I did. Perhaps God miraculously intervened in their lives too. I will never know. What I do know is that Jesus Himself came into my life in the spiritual world, saved me from death, and walked me back out into life. That is a miracle. I was asleep. I was vulnerable. I was exhausted. I was a prime target for the devil, and he had me. I could do nothing on my own. Only through the miraculous, saving work of Jesus was I spared. Yes, God still does miracles in our time...and even in America.

Still, most often, it seems we need some additional help in the physical world, and God is there to help us with that too. I needed the loving and yet engaged "kick your butt" approach of my angel of Blue respiratory nurse. Anything less, and I may not have made it through. God knew exactly what I needed and provided it. Even more, in the enormous hospital I was in, He paved the way for my angel of Blue to follow me from the ICU up to my regular hospital room. She saw me literally to the finish line. We became friends through this process and are still connected today. While we may have differences (what friends don't?), we share a love for Jesus, and we share this story. I think my success story was good for her too. Not just the success but because she often had patients who did not make it. I'm sure that was heartbreaking for her and thousands of other medical providers throughout the COVID pandemic. Like anyone, you like to see the fruits of your labors, and seeing people pass away must have been a kick in the gut.

One time while she was checking on me, her husband called. It was a video call, and she wanted him to meet me. We spoke for a few minutes, and I thanked him multiple times for allowing this angel to leave home and be used by God in Texas to help...me. He said she had spoken of a patient that was headed in the right direction. A patient with a certain joy, peace, and love that can only be explained by a love for Jesus. After that call ended, I told her I had only seen her eyes during our time together. That is all I had seen of anyone since arriving at the hospital, except for when my wife visited me. I said that she had seen my face, but I didn't even know what she looked like. She pulled her mask down for a brief moment so I could see the face of my angel of Blue. I will not forget it.

I also learned during this time that God can bring peace to us in unexpected ways. For me, it was the nightly pigeon parade. Before this experience, I didn't think too much about pigeons. I see them sometimes, like most other people, but aside from being funny, they're more annoying than anything. But on that first night in my regular room, God used them to take my mind off me and my situation. I entered their world for a brief time. It gave me peace to simply wonder why they do the things they do and, as I discovered the next morning, where they go all day. Indeed, God does not need some fantastic sign in the heavens or an audible voice to give you a sense of peace. He can even use some pigeons.

I learned many lessons during this time, but perhaps the biggest lesson I learned is just how precious life truly is. In God's way of doing things, we only get one life on this earth. We all get a life after that and are free to choose where and with whom we get to live it. That life is our eternal life and the most important one, but as we are temporal beings who can't fully understand that eternal life, we focus on the one life we have on this earth. And that life is precious. Not only do we have the opportunity to love God during that life, but we also get the opportunity to love other people and be loved by them. We get the opportunity to glorify God through the talents He gives us, through our work, our resources, our words, and our actions. We have the opportunity to live well and die surrounded by many people or to not live well and be surrounded by a few.

Jesus brought me back from the brink and gave me a second chance. I hope and pray that I will live that second chance well. I hope and pray that I will do well with the one life opportunity He has given me. What will you do with the one life opportunity He has given you?

Chapter Two

Meanwhile, Back at the Ranch...

(This was not the journey of a man but instead the journey of a family. This story could not be fully told without the perspective of my wife, Melissa. Here is her journey in her own words)

"Whenever I am afraid, I will trust in You" (Psalm 56:3 NKJV). I found myself repeating this verse to the kids when they shared fears and concerns as their dad was fighting for his life. I was saying it to myself, wondering what I would do if the worst happened. It brought to reality just why we are called to hide God's Word in our hearts. That verse was buried there from childhood when I memorized it in Bible class in school or at a church Vacation Bible School. It was there when I needed it. God's Word hidden in my heart for just the moment I was struggling. Truth that I used for weeks on end to calm myself and my children as their dad was fighting to regain his strength.

Fear is powerful, but for the Christian, it is irrational. We are saved and redeemed by the Creator; fear has no place in His presence. During this time, we strove to hold on to the truth of who God is and who we are as His children. We were made to be fearless because we belong to the Almighty.

When Darrin told me to call for an ambulance, I was relieved. Relieved for many different reasons, but the main one being that if we took him to the ER near us, it was connected to the urgent care that had not taken proper care of him in the first place. We were new to the area and had no idea where the "real" hospital was. We were all packed up to go on our trip to the hospital when he told me he couldn't bear the thought of sitting in a waiting room and wanted me to call for an ambulance. It took it out of my control when he made that decision. He is a decisive person, and even as a very sick man he remained decisive.

As I called 9-1-1, I felt a calm come over me. The woman on the call asked me a few questions and seemed shocked by my answers. I assured her that my husband was indeed conscious and that, no, his lips were not blue. Apparently, his oxygen level was so low that it was amazing to her these things were not happening. She offered to stay on the call with me if I needed it, but I thanked her and told her there was no need. Before she hung up, she asked that the kids and I wear masks when the ambulance arrived.

Before we masked up, we prayed together. Over the years, that has been our first response in situations of great weight. It really began when Darrin was a police officer. I would pray over him before each shift, and it gave me peace knowing he was in God's hands as he faced the dangers of the day (or night, depending on the shift he was working). Give it to God, or in this case, give him to God.

After we prayed, we said goodbye to each other. We knew he would most likely be gone for the night, at least. Darrin sprang into "information mode" and reminded me of where the life insurance papers were. This was the last thing I wanted to hear or think about. He was coming home, I told him, and I had no need for that information now. "Stay positive." "Get better." Those were the things I wanted in his mind, not how we would survive without him.

The firefighters arrived and immediately helped Darrin feel so much better. As the ambulance arrived, things went into high gear. They strapped him on a stretcher and gave us a moment for another quick goodbye. Savannah and Schuyler were real troopers. They hugged their dad goodbye as they held back tears. They instinctively knew that crying would cause their dad to cry too, which would not be good for him right now. They encouraged him to get better and that they would be helpful while he was gone.

As I told Darrin goodbye one last time, I focused on what was needed *of* me at that moment. I kept my mind busy focusing on what he needed rather than what I was feeling. I smiled from under my mask and told him to get better. Miraculously, I was able to see him out the door without tears.

Once Darrin was on his way to the ambulance, the doctor who had arrived first with the firefighters returned to speak with me. I was relieved to see him coming back because, in all the hustle and bustle, I had no idea where they were taking him. When he got to the door, I quickly asked what hospital Darrin would be taken to. This man realized then that I was not understanding the gravity of the situation and what our hospital stay timeframe would look like. He told me where they were going but cautioned me that Darrin would be there for a long time.

After speaking with that doctor, I must have taken the picture of our children watching their dad being loaded into the ambulance. Honestly, I don't remember taking the picture. The kids always waved goodbye as Darrin would leave for work, so it was natural to wave as he left in the ambulance. They stood there long after the ambulance was out of sight, not wanting to miss another chance to see their dad.

As we closed the front door, the tears began to fall. Our world felt like it was crashing in. We had all played our part in keeping Darrin's spirits lifted, and now we could let it hit us like the ton of bricks it was. We were alone and without our protector, yet God was there. Our earthly protector was gone, but our ever-present heavenly Protector never moved. God used the moments and days to come to remind all of us that He will never leave us nor forsake us. I allowed myself one breakdown. I cried so hard that first night. I called my mom and let it all out. How was I going to do it all?!

By this point, I was the last one in our family to get sick. Both kids had felt tired and under the weather and had already recovered by the time Darrin went to the hospital. On the other hand, I was in the middle of my illness. I had been so busy with Darrin and the kids that I had been pushing through. But now I was exhausted. My mom reminded me that with Darrin being cared for by professionals, I would be able to rest and get better too. God was giving us all rest and care. My mom is a wise woman. Still, calls had to be made. Texts had to be sent. My pity party had to be over. After everyone was notified, all we could do was pray...and wait.

The first update call came that night from the ICU doctor. He let me know that Darrin was being assessed and would be in the ICU for at least a few nights. He said they would put him on a ventilator...the line went dead! We had been disconnected. They put my husband on a ventilator!? My phone rang again. It was the hospital. The doctor said he was sorry, but the phone in the ICU had a bad cord and was known to cut a call off. Oh, great! I immediately asked him to please repeat the part about the ventilator because the call dropped as he mentioned it. Was Darrin on a ventilator? He assured me that Darrin was very sick but was NOT on a ventilator. Praise the Lord! What he had been saying was that they would try their best to keep him off the ventilator, but if he did need to be put on a vent, they would call to let me know. The ICU doctor told me that I would be called daily by whoever was on call to update me on how Darrin was progressing.

That night, as I finally laid my head on my pillow, I could see the moon so bright out our bedroom window. As I looked up at it, I felt God say, "I'm here. I still see you. You aren't alone." Covid was such a lonely time for so many and now it would spread its loneliness to us. I felt so terribly alone that first night. God knew I needed to know He was right there with me. To this day, if I see the moon shining brightly in my window as I go to bed, I thank God for the visual reminder that He is always with me.

The first morning after Darrin was taken to the hospital, I was awakened by calls and texts for updates. I had nothing new to tell. I hadn't spoken to the hospital since my first call from the ICU. Darrin had his phone with him and was able to send me brief text updates, but the next official call from the hospital wasn't until late in the afternoon that first day. The physician's assistant I spoke with became my lifeline and trusted source of information while Darrin was in the ICU. Sarah (as Darrin has called her) was matter-of-fact, and yet so comforting in her updates. She was patient as I asked questions and encouraging as she conveyed everything they were doing to help Darrin get better.

For eleven days, that was my life. I was waking up to requests for updates on Darrin and waiting for information to fulfill those requests. The waiting. Always waiting. That is something I will never forget. There was comfort in not having a middle-of-the-night update because that meant everything was still all right, but the waiting was stressful. Why wasn't I getting an update yet? Did someone forget to call me? What if everything WASN'T okay and I just didn't know yet!? Every day seemed filled with the same worried thoughts.

Yet every day, God gave me peace. His reminders came in the words of Bible verses and songs of praise. "But those who wait on the Lord shall renew their strength; they shall mount up with wings like eagles, they shall run and not be weary, they shall walk and not faint" (Isaiah 40:31 NKJV). "Salvation belongs to our God, who sits on the throne, and to the Lamb" (Revelation 7:10 NIV). Verses and promises like this flooded my heart and mind. God was so good to me during this time. I was very alone, in a state far from our families, yet God provided friendships in Texas that will last this lifetime and into eternity. Christian friends that were there for our family every step of the journey to get Darrin back to health. Friends that provided help, meals, and encouragement; they were the hands and feet of Jesus to us during this time.

I was able to visit Darrin once he was out of the ICU and in a regular hospital room. In order to visit him, I had to find a place to leave our kids for a few hours. One of our dear friends offered to take care of them for me while I visited him. Her generosity made it possible for me to see my husband after a week apart. Our reunion was one to remember. The only reunion better than that one was when he was released to come home.

When I received Darrin's call that he would be released from the hospital, we rushed right over. After three hours of waiting for him to come out of the hospital, we could finally see him being pushed out the doors in a wheelchair. This was the first time Savannah and Schuyler had seen him in eleven days. He was thinner and pale...and he was on oxygen. They were so happy to see their dad but also a little apprehensive. This man was a different man than we had sent off to the hospital. How different was yet to be seen.

The man who came home with us was grateful to be alive but fearful to live. Leaving the hospital was what he wanted, but being at home was far from the comfort he expected. Almost as soon as we "crept" from the van to the front door, his strength was completely spent. Standing up alone took all he could give. He was panicky while we set up his portable oxygen tank and removed the travel tank he came home with. Fear of the tank being accidentally turned off was so real to him that the kids made a sign to attach to the machine – "Do NOT Turn Off!!!" The sound of the machine soon began to calm his nerves, and it became a constant background sound for weeks to come.

The weeks that came after he arrived home were filled with joy and frustration. Darrin was home, and that was enough to shoulder any burden or jump over any hurdle.

But caring for your spouse is a strange thing. There is a delicate balance to maintain dignity and respect. I needed him to feel like the man of our house. I needed him to feel seen by me as my husband and partner in life. I needed him to WANT to get better. So, while I helped and cared for him, I also encouraged and enabled him to take care of himself in ways that he could. Eating off a plate was hard for him at first. He was at a tv tray on the couch and the plate was heavy to hold, so we put food in cups. It was a challenge to keep our household stocked with clean cups during this phase, but it enabled him to be able to eat and feel independent without feeling like he was making a mess. A win for all of us!

He would get winded so easily, even with the oxygen on, that I found myself stopping what I was doing numerous times throughout the day to calm him as he would catch his breath. Patience was my lesson during this time. Slowing down was what was needed for both of us so that he could catch his breath, and so I could remember how blessed I was that he was alive and home with me. These moments were precious and still remind us of the ebb and flow of a beautiful relationship...to carry and be carried.

Stretching his comfort zone was a bit of a struggle. Darrin has always been one for routines, and his recovery was no different. He was getting used to relying on me to assist in everyday things, but I could see he was getting stronger and should try to do things without the safety net of me standing there beside him. We had settled into a comfortable routine where I accompanied him everywhere he went in the house, but it was time to branch out a bit.

The weather was beautiful for November (remember we were living in Texas), so the kids and I often sat outside enjoying the sunshine of autumn. This would be the perfect next step for a man who had only left the house one time for a follow-up doctor's visit. I suggested sitting with me out on the porch for a little bit. I told Darrin the sun and fresh air would do him good, and he reminded me that "cedar fever" was still a real thing. This was going to be more difficult than I had expected.

I got his oxygen hose stretched out to make sure it could reach comfortably outside, and then I suggested he just try it. I opened the door and walked with him to the backyard. With his anxiety, you would think we had stepped out of a spaceship onto the surface of Mars. He sat down in a chair, caught his breath (which was taking less time now), and relaxed. As we sat there looking and listening to the world outside the walls of the house, I could see him start to wriggle free from fear's grip a little more. He was enjoying being outside again, and over the next few weeks, I would often look out the window and see him relaxing on the porch.

When he didn't need supplemental oxygen anymore, Darrin began to feel more able. He was getting stronger. He was doing more things and taking more risks. Of course, as a man, it was time to push things too far.

Before we were to leave for Christmas break, Darrin wanted the lawn to be mowed one more time. I had been keeping the grass cut since he had been sick, but now that he was feeling better, he kept suggesting he could do it himself. We had a long trip ahead of us to visit family, so I told him that I thought it would be best if I did the yard, and he could weed whip the edges. He agreed.

He started edging the yard while I finished some packing. I opened the front door as he began edging just in case he needed help. Through the glass storm door I could see him feeling accomplished as he worked. I packed quickly, hoping to get out there and get the yard mowed before he grew impatient. That's when I heard a lawn mower. He wouldn't! Yep, there he was, grinning from ear to ear as he walked back and forth cutting the grass. I stepped outside, and he shut off the mower. He said he felt fine and wanted to cut the small portion of grass we had in our front yard. I objected, but he was firm in his resolve. He wasn't my child but my husband. I couldn't really stop him.

After 15 minutes or so things got very quiet outside. During this time, Savannah and Schuyler had grown accustomed to listening for Darrin. They often heard him call me before I ever did. This time was no exception. He hadn't called for me...yet...but because they heard the same quiet outside, they went out to the garage to investigate. There they found their dad, out of breath, asking them to "get Mom." Savannah rushed in and alerted me that Darrin needed my help. Apparently, not one to show outward upset, I calmly but quickly walked to the garage. There he sat, looking sheepishly at me. He wasn't ready to mow the grass yet, but after he recovered, he picked up the weed whip and edged the rest of the yard while I mowed. A slight setback, but really a victory. Through this, he realized that while he wasn't yet one hundred percent, he was a lot stronger than a month before.

This time was strangely akin to parenting, except this was my spouse. The encouraging had to be empowering because I was helping rebuild a man, not grow a boy into a man. My words and actions had to convey the need that I had to see our family's leader return, without adding stress or shame as he regained his strength. This was quite a journey, but the small steps of regaining independence quickly rebuilt his confidence, and then...he was back!

God never promised us a smooth, easy life when we give our hearts to Him, but He does promise to "never leave you nor forsake you" (Hebrews 13:5b NKJV). I can tell you that is true. Jesus was all I had during those eleven days, and He was more than enough. He helped me through Darrin's recovery at home also. If our story ended differently than this, would I be so sure He was more than enough? Yes, I would. My heart would be broken as I write this. It would not be filled with the happiness of knowing my husband and I have more time on this earth to still enjoy together, but Jesus would still be Lord. I had such peace knowing that if God allowed Darrin to pass on to eternity, he was ready. I could have never felt the peace I found if I had been unsure of Darrin's salvation.

I'm so thankful our story didn't end with that quick goodbye before he was wheeled out to the ambulance. I still thank God for the small moments I get to share with my husband and our kids get to spend with their dad. It is easy to forget how it felt to be that close to losing him, but I don't want to ever lose that feeling. That feeling is a reminder to be forgiving and loving and to live each day as if tomorrow may not come...because tomorrow is surely not promised.

Chapter Three

Picture Pages

Head on over to www.backfromthebrinkbook.com to see all the pictures mentioned in this book. You will also find information on an upcoming opportunity to join with Darrin in fighting for the freedom and liberty of future generations in the United States of America. See you there!